*Children's Dreaming
and the
Development of Consciousness*

Children's Dreaming

and the

Development of Consciousness

~

David Foulkes

Harvard University Press

CAMBRIDGE, MASSACHUSETTS
LONDON, ENGLAND
1999

Library of Congress Cataloging-in-Publication Data

Foulkes, David, 1935–
Children's dreaming and the development of consciousness / David
Foulkes.
p.   cm.
Includes bibliographical references and index.
ISBN 0-674-11620-8 (alk. paper)
1. Children's dreams.   2. Consciousness.   I. Title.
BF1099.C55F67   1999
154.6'3'083—dc21   98-26307

For Nancy

Contents

~

Children's Dreaming
and the
Development of Consciousness

~

Introduction

~

This book describes and interprets findings from research conducted over the past several decades on the extent and nature of dreaming in children from ages 3 to 15. They are in many respects startling and challenge a number of our deepest beliefs about both the process of dreaming and the nature of children's inner experience. Specifically, these findings suggest that dreaming is a symbolic production neither generally shared with other animals nor generally present in early childhood, and that reflective consciousness itself, therefore, is neither generally shared with other animals nor generally present in early childhood.

The basic dream findings documented here are as yet little known, whether by the general reading public or by professionals in cognitive studies or in the neuro-sciences. They are not found in most popular writing or other expositions on dreaming. They are absent in textbooks of general or developmental psychology.

In part, perhaps, this neglect was fostered by their original appearance in one formidable book (Foulkes, 1982a) that included 150 pages of technical appendices, and in subsequent articles in two technical journals not generally read by mainstream academic psychologists (Foulkes, Hollifield, Sullivan,

Bradley, & Terry, 1990; Foulkes, Hollifield, Bradley, Terry, & Sullivan, 1991). But the neglect also may reflect the unwillingness of both professionals and the general public to believe that a scientific approach to children's dreaming is either possible or likely to produce any truly important results.

To study children's dreaming scientifically would mean, in the first instance, making careful observations of dream phenomena under the best possible conditions, and just when the child has been awakened from the experience, and then it would mean standardizing both the inquiries one makes of the child and the numerical summarization and statistical treatment of the data supplied by the dreamer. Thanks to the discovery of REM (*R*apid *E*ye *M*ovement) sleep in the early 1950s (Aserinsky & Kleitman, 1953), and the subsequent elaboration of sleep-laboratory methods for nighttime dream collection (Dement & Kleitman, 1957), dreams now can be sampled representatively and with minimal distortion by subsequent waking memory processes. Thanks to the relatively recent development of rating and content-analysis systems for summarizing observations of both the form and the substance of dream experience (see Hall & Van de Castle, 1966; Winget & Kramer, 1979; Domhoff, 1996), reliable analysis of dream data now is possible. That is, multiple observers who examine the same dreams can make the same summary statements of them and draw the same conclusions.

Scientific observation of children's early dream life is not only important to those interested in dreaming as such. When we ask children to tell us their dreams, we are asking them to describe and characterize a conscious mental state. Never mind that the child may still believe that it is real, rather than mental, events that he or she is talking about. The larger importance of dream reports is that they offer an unparalleled opportunity to learn if and when young children can experience conscious mental states and what kind of conscious mental states they can, and cannot, experience.

Ample evidence from human neuropsychology demonstrates that adult dream consciousness parallels adult waking consciousness. For instance, if, because of selective brain damage, the visual form of mental imagery cannot be experienced while awake, then it also cannot be experienced when asleep. We have no good reason to doubt that similar waking-dreaming parallels hold during early development as well. This would mean that, in reporting dreams, young children are doing something it is well near impossible to get them to do under any other circumstance: they are telling us about their ability to experience *conscious* cognitive states.

The results described here, then, give us our first scientifically reliable picture of the nature of dreaming in early childhood, and they also afford the best opportunity now available to determine when and how children first begin to experience conscious mental states. From birth, we surely can credit children with sensitivity to environmental and organic stimuli, but when are they first capable not only of seeing X but also of being conscious of seeing X? I will try to demonstrate that dreaming of X must be exactly the same kind of experience as the waking consciousness of seeing X, and that dream competence can therefore be used to index the development of the waking capacity to experience conscious states.

The dream data used here come from a 20-year program of research on dreaming, from preschool to high-school years.

The program comprised, along with some other briefer projects, two major studies. One was longitudinal, that is, the same children were followed over time as they grew up (Foulkes, 1982a). The other was cross-sectional, that is, age comparisons were made using different groups of children (Foulkes, Hollifield, Sullivan, Bradley, & Terry, 1990; Foulkes, Hollifield, Bradley, Terry, & Sullivan, 1991). The two studies produced precisely the same pattern of results, a pattern I did not originally anticipate but one that does make a new and interesting kind of sense.

Unlike the plethora of popular books on dreaming currently available, this one is heavily constrained by reliable empirical observation. That should make it more trustworthy, but not, I hope, more difficult to read. In the interest of reaching out to as wide an audience as possible, I have tried to write nontechnically, without sacrificing essential accuracy. Since the dream findings themselves have been published before in a much more detailed format, the interested reader has the opportunity to check how well I have succeeded in this, and to find there further quantitative documentation for claims made here.

The astute reader will note that the first terms of the title of this book refer to children's dreaming, and not to their dreams. Although the study of *how* children dream and of *what* they dream do have a common starting point in the data base of children's dream reports, there is an important difference in emphasis. The reason for my emphasis here on process, rather than on content, is that the findings of systematic research on children's dreams have far more interesting things to say about the mind that does the dreaming than about the dream itself.

Specifically, I hope to show that my data on dream development have significant implications for what has heretofore been one of the imponderables of human developmental psychology: the development of consciousness.

Because of its focus on the process of dreaming, my account may be too generalized for some readers, who will long for *examples* of particular children's dreams. I therefore have included an appendix that abstracts all of the REM dreams reported by two children in the longitudinal study. The younger child, Dean, reported his dreams from ages 4 to 9, while the older child, Emily (not their real names), reported hers from ages 10 to 15. As with any individual data, these two dream series don't illustrate all of the developments I describe, but they do reflect most of them, and give a concrete appreciation for the age trends that are the subject of this book.

But my first task here is to examine the expectations that my novel and possibly counterintuitive findings on children's dreams seem to violate, and to answer the question whether flaws in my own methods could be responsible for the discrepancies between my findings and such expectations.

1

Challenging the Assumptions

Most people (including many psychologists) with whom I have talked seem to believe that dreaming is a "given" in human experience. It has always been there, even in infancy, in pretty much the form that we know it now. Many, of course, also impute dreaming to other animals. It is easy to believe, as we watch a pet dog "chasing rabbits" while sleeping on a rug in front of the fireplace, that dreaming is some sort of elementary activity, widely shared across species and having no particular nor very stringent cognitive prerequisites. And if that is the case, why shouldn't human infants dream as well?

It isn't too long after birth that we see behavioral signs during sleep even in the motorically inept human—smiles, sighs, cries—that we readily attribute to dreaming. Later on, of course, there will be speech fragments that seem even more unequivocally to index some inner mental experience during sleep. And finally, there is the discovery that REM sleep, known in the adult to support our most vivid and elaborate dreaming, is not only present in infants, but present in greater degree in neonates, and especially in prematures, than at any other point in the human life cycle (see Feinberg, 1969).

Both critical and empirical analyses, however, make it appear much less certain that human infants are capable of dreaming. Our dreams are conscious experiences woven from our particular memories and general knowledge. The first problem for the proponent of infantile dreaming is, what could be the dream content when there is little or no prior world information from which to build dreams? One possibility, of course, is that, when there is little background or stored information available, then dreams use currently present sensory stimuli as source material. A famous developmental psychologist once assured me that the fetus dreams of perturbations in its intrauterine environment. But if infantile dreaming is driven externally rather than internally, it is certainly very different from our dreaming, which we know, from extensive attempts to modify REM-dream reports by experimentally delivered stimuli, is relatively impervious to external influence and certainly in no way dependent on external stimuli (see, for instance, reviews in Arkin, Antrobus, & Ellman, 1978). External stimuli are, in fact, actively occluded during REM sleep (Rechtschaffen & Foulkes, 1965).

Another possible source of infantile dreaming might lie in inherited mental complexes, such as Jung's (1960) "archetypes"—a collective kind of knowledge that is only later overlaid with individual experience and knowledge. The problem here, put simply, is that there is no reliable evidence for such complexes, and that the only motivation for proposing them is to prejudge the issue by simply assuming a rich infantile memory and the consequent possibility of a rich infantile dream life.

But the larger conceptual problem with infantile dreaming is not *of* what the infant could be dreaming but *with* what the infant could be dreaming. Our dreams, whatever their sources, are, as we now know from REM-dream studies (see Foulkes, 1985), generally coherent and internally plausible images strung together over time as generally coherent and internally plausible narrative sequences. They are *not*, as the stereotype has it, illogical sequences of bizarre images—that stereotype rests, if there is any evidence for it at all, on the biased samples we get from dreams that happen to awaken us. Representative sampling of dreams, now made possible by monitoring REM sleep and systematic awakenings from it, indicates that dream imagery and sequences are generally well formed.

And so we have the problem, and it is an especially big problem if the sources of infantile dreams are imagined to lie in haphazard stimulation from the environment, of explaining how the newborn or young infant could manage to make coherent experiences or stories out of its dream sources. That is a level of infantile symbolic skill for which we have no waking evidence. Why should, and how could, it be present in sleep?

There is an obvious fallback position here. OK, infants' dreams are different from ours, they are probably more dependent on the external environment and less coherent than our own, but infants still do (or must) dream some kind of dream. Note, however, in terms of the original argument, that this concession is considerable. It no longer is the case that dreaming is the same across the life span; now it is allowed that dreaming *develops*, and that it does so in some sort of accord with waking mental development. That makes dreaming something very different from the "given" of the original argument, and it raises questions about the supposed prevalence of dreaming in other species.

Another fallback position that I have encountered (and this for much older children as well for infants) is that infants and children often may be dreaming but are not yet *conscious* of their dreams. This position is, at best, misleading, and ultimately nonsensical. We know, from the evidence of REM sleep (or indeed that of any normal sleep stage), that the brain is electrophysiologically active, that "information," in the neural sense, is being processed. But that is not "dreaming." Even if information were being processed in the cognitive sense (such that, following REM sleep, one could demonstrate behaviorally a reorganization of memory networks), that would surely be an interesting datum for cognitive psychology, but it would not necessarily have a single thing to do with dreaming. Dreaming is, *by definition*, conscious experience—it is the awareness of being in an imagined world in which things happen. Whatever else happens during REM sleep—either electrophysiologically or in the so-called "cognitive unconscious" where the mind processes information outside our awareness—that is *not* dreaming, and, in fact, despite fecund theorizing, absolutely nothing is known at present about *that activity's relation* to dreaming.

Empirically, there are additional problems with the casual assumption that there must be infantile dreaming. It is true that compared to adults, infants have much REM sleep, and that REM sleep in the adult is frequently accompanied by extended dream episodes. But the association of REM sleep with dreaming in the adult does not necessarily imply that that relation also holds true in infancy or in other animals. The adult association, moreover, is as yet cloaked in neurobiological ignorance. What particular features of REM sleep, neurophysiologically described, might be responsible for the association with dreaming? Are *they* present in equal form in infants and other species as in the adult human? We don't know. Is what we call REM sleep in the infant and in other species exactly like REM sleep in the adult human? Likely not. In such circumstances, extreme caution probably should be observed in generalizing from one observational context to others.

Laboratory research also suggests caution in believing that conscious *experience* must underlie *behavior* during sleep, or during REM sleep. For the adult who can reliably report the mental experience that accompanied his or her observable behavior during sleep, the relationship of behavior to reported experience is quite imperfect. Sleepwalkers almost never seem to be acting out a dream (see Jacobson, Kales, Lehmann, & Zweizig, 1965) and sleep-talking from the same deep non-REM stage of sleep from which walking most commonly is initiated is very rarely related to ongoing dream conversation (Arkin, 1981). In this sleep stage, behavior most likely is not actively stimulated but under passive release from its usual inhibition. At any rate, its indexing of mental content ranges from poor to nonexistent.

In lighter sleep stages (including REM), there is a somewhat better, but still imperfect, relation between sleep speech and dream speech (Arkin, 1981). Even here it is not clear that speech production is an integral part of the dreaming process; it may be independent of dream construction until the point when the speech is heard, and then incorporated as if it were any other external stimulus. In that case, the speech would index dreaming insofar as the dreamer has a mind capable of weaving external stimuli into an ongoing dream narrative, which is precisely what we don't know about young children, infants, or dogs.

In the face of these conceptual and empirical problems, the persistence with which the possibility of infantile (and animal) dreaming is defended stems in large measure from an implicit equation of dreaming with perception. If an organism gives evidence that it can perceive a reality, then we are prone to imagine that it can dream one as well.

On reflection, however, it seems likely that there is a big difference between seeing the real world and seeing a dream world. Whatever one's ultimate philosophical position might be, there is a clear everyday sense in which perception reflects patterned information presented to the senses. But dreaming creates patterns that have never been experienced before, and it does so in the absence of environmental stimulation. Indeed, much of the literature on infantile waking cognition makes this distinction: infants can manipulate information currently available in the environment, but they cannot manipulate information without concurrent environmental support. In effect, they can "think" of dolly when it's there, but not when it's not. How, then, could they not only conjure up a picture of dolly, but also make up a story about dolly while sleeping?

Furthermore, it is not even clear that infantile perception is like what we think of as prototypic perception. Our typical idea of "perception" is that I see X and that I am aware that I am seeing X. It is like my state of mind when I am driving, focused on the road, and try to determine if the object ahead is a branch or a cat, rather than like when I'm driving (still quite adequately, as it usually turns out) while preoccupied and not consciously aware of the passing scene. Suppose, not implausibly (Weiskrantz, 1997, p. 166), that visually guided behavior in the infant is more like the latter case than the former. Then the infant's "perception" is not conscious in the sense that we imagine ours mostly to be, and it would seem to provide little basis for the kind of consciousness that we experience while we dream.

My assumption here is that the term "consciousness" is most appropriately applied in psychology to a phenomenon that is inherently reflective. There is an enormous literature outside of psychology (philosophy, neurosciences, "neurophilosophy") dealing with the more problematic and mysterious aspects of consciousness, for instance: how the material brain, which has location, mass, and volume, can generate or be associated with consciousness, which seems to have none of these properties (the "mind-body" problem); what kind of thing or process consciousness is (the "nature of consciousness" problem); and whether computers or other artificial systems have, or might someday have, conscious mental states. In this tradition, conceptual analysis and "thought experiments" are typical methodologies.

In experimental psychology, on the other hand, although philosophical and neuroscientific analyses remain influential, real experimentation is more abundant. The primary issue has been to determine the functional differences between behavior that is accessible to self-reflection, self-report, and self-recollection, and behavior that does not have these properties. There is much evidence to suggest that in this sense, consciousness does make a difference; that is, conscious processing is different from nonconscious processing and has different functional consequences.

Experimental distinctions between *declarative* and *procedural* memory (Squire, 1986) and between *explicit* and *implicit* memory (Schacter, 1987) build on this difference. Developmental evidence indicates that this difference may be critical in evaluating cognitive differences between infancy and later development (Moscovitch, 1984). Neuropsychological studies of human brain damage have shown, especially in cases of amnesia and blindsight (Weiskrantz, 1997), that capacities we normally would assume to be consciously mediated can be accomplished without awareness, and researchers have identified systematic differences between conscious and nonconscious processing.

In defining "consciousness" as a self-reflective act, psychology loses much of the glamour and mystery of other areas of consciousness-study, but it also can proceed on a workaday basis without becoming paralyzed in pure abstraction. And it does, I think, end up with a concept of consciousness that is both reasonably close to that of everyday usage and reasonably susceptible to empirical study.

For example, most of us, I believe, would not want to say that mere responsiveness is a sufficient condition of consciousness. Plants, for example, may fold their leaves in response to human touch. We generally do not believe plants to be conscious (although Robert Macnish's *The Philosophy of Sleep* [1834] does include a brief chapter on "Sleep of Plants").

Being "awake" is sometimes cited as a condition of consciousness, but there are everyday objections to this specification as well, including, on the one hand, that we can be "awake," at least physiologically, yet momentarily not be conscious of anything at all, and, on the other hand, that we are conscious of dream events while we are in fact not awake, but asleep. In addition, sleep researchers have found it difficult even to define wakefulness in some lower vertebrates, much less invertebrates, where self-report obviously is impossible and where the creature's underlying physiology may be quite different from our own.

Being "mentally" responsive is sometimes advanced as a sufficient condition of consciousness. But it is not at all clear what operations could reasonably define mental responsiveness. Do we simply define such responsiveness in terms of a certain kind of nervous system or other physiological mediation, such that we arbitrarily seem to decide which creatures are capable of mental or cognitive response to their environment, and which not? Besides, there is still the problem that, in the driving example from my everyday experience, I seemed to be mentally/cognitively responsive to, while I was not conscious of, where I was driving.

The equation of consciousness with self-reflection I am proposing, and which experimental psychology has at least in part embraced, is not without support within the more abstract philosophical tradition. One contender among the various schools of philosophical thought is the HOT theory, namely, the idea that consciousness necessarily involves Higher-Order Thought (Gennaro, 1996). As David Rosenthal puts it, "a mental state's being conscious is its being accompanied by a roughly simultaneous higher-order thought about that very mental state" (1993, p. 198).

By this definition of consciousness, much adult cognition is nonconscious: we set ourselves a problem, and then the solution appears, but we are unable to identify the mental processes or operations that generated it. Mental processes often are unobserved, and unobservable. The failure of pure introspection to solve the riddles of human cognition around the turn of the twentieth century may be accounted for precisely by the nonobservable (by the self)—and hence nonreportable—nature of much of our cognitive processing (Humphrey, 1951). Also on this definition, infant consciousness seems relatively unlikely.

This digression on consciousness was initiated by a concern about whether human perception and conscious cognition (such as dreaming) are comparable in nature. Fortunately, there is empirical evidence on this question, evidence that establishes their difference from one another, and, in the process, shows that dreaming is continuous with our waking *reflective ability to think in images* rather than with our waking perceptual competence (Kerr, 1993).

First, we have evidence (see Kerr, Foulkes, & Schmidt, 1982) from the dreams of persons adventitiously blinded after ages 5 to 7 (and these very ages will later be shown to be critical in the development of dreaming in the sighted). These people, by definition, no longer see or can barely see. But they continue to be able while awake to conjure up mental images of persons, objects, and events, and they continue to dream in imagery. Interestingly, they can both think and dream visual imagery of persons or events that happened since their blinding, that is, which they never experienced visually in the first place.

Blinding at earlier ages than 5 to 7 is associated with the subsequent absence of both waking visualization in thought and of visual dreaming. The importance of the period from age 5 to 7 in maintaining visual dreaming is well established, and has been known in the scientific literature for a century now (Jastrow, 1900). What it clearly suggests is that in the span between these ages, whatever rudimentary imaging might have occurred earlier now becomes transformed into a semipermanent system which is almost wholly independent of the possibility of concurrent perceptual processing. Visualization of the fluid sort that we find in our dreams is a *thought process* wholly severed from whatever sort of dependence it once might have had on direct perceptual experience.

Cases of selective cognitive impairment in adult patients with brain lesions make the same general point. Even when the patient continues to see, if there is impairment of waking mental visualization, there invariably is comparable impairment in dreaming. And if there is impairment of dreaming, there invariably is comparable impairment, not in seeing but in being able visually to imagine (see the review by Kerr, 1993). Functionally, our kind of dreaming is related, not to how we see, but to how we are able to think about persons, objects, and events when they are not physically present.

My argument thus far has been that the received wisdom that human infants (and other animals) dream stands on very shaky ground, both conceptually and, more importantly, empirically. But the argument has been roundabout rather than direct. Much of the reason for this is obvious: we can't ask infants (or other animals, although it's been tried: Vaughan, 1963 [compare Foulkes, 1983]) simply to tell us about their dream life, if any. But we could begin asking 3- and 4-year-olds about their dreams, and by seeing what the situation was there, make some informed backward projections to earlier ages.

You might imagine, however, that such a project would be fraught with perils: how do we know that the children even understand what a "dream" is? how do we know that a child actually is telling us one? how can we study children in ways that are objective enough to be uncontaminated by their suggestibility and their desire to tell us what they think we want to hear, but that still give them the support and encouragement needed to facilitate genuine reporting? The seeming insuperability of these and other problems did not totally deter research on the dream reports of young children, but such research, before the discovery of REM sleep, had not established any generally reliable findings (DeMartino, 1955). (This likewise was the case with adult dream research before the discovery of REM sleep: Ramsey, 1953.)

Shortly after the development of laboratories for the study of REM dreaming, there were a few efforts at working with children (Kohler, Coddington, & Agnew, 1968; Kales, Kales, Jacobson, Po, & Green, 1968), but no systematic program of research. Finally, in the mid 1960s, I rushed in where others feared to tread (see Foulkes, Pivik, Steadman, Spear, & Symonds, 1967; Foulkes, 1967; Foulkes, Larson, Swanson, & Rardin, 1969). An investigator faces many choices in studying children's dream life, and I intend to explain and justify mine; most critically, why I studied children in a sleep laboratory instead of at home or in school (typical choices of earlier investigators).

2

~

How to Study Children's Dreams

At first, the task doesn't sound difficult: if you want to find out about children's dreams, just ask them. But *who* should ask them, and *how*, and *when*, and *where?* Failure to reflect adequately on these seemingly nagging little details has been responsible for considerable confusion in research and thinking on children's dream life.

The Justification of Sleep-Laboratory Methods

Let's begin with the "who" question. Prime candidates most often are considered to be either children's parents (the first choice) or children's teachers or other figures from the preschool or school. The parents are considered (even in today's climate of "dysfunctional" family life) to be closest to their children, and to have the sort of rapport that encourages disclosure and the kind of judgment that allows for the best evaluation of what children tell them. Teachers and other school figures may come up somewhat shorter on rapport, but they have the advantage of working in an environment that, at least traditionally, shapes and encourages accuracy in reporting.

But many factors argue against parents as collectors of their children's dream reports. It is generally believed that children learn the concept of "dream" when they present some improbable account of an overnight occurrence to their parents, who respond with something like "Oh, you must have *dreamed* that. That was only a *dream*." In fact the parents' role is likely to be much more directive than that. Middle-class parents (those whose children are by far the most likely participants in any dream project) will jump the gun. They will be watching and waiting for their children's dream life to unfold, and, along the way, they will be ministering potent suggestions to their children about what their dreams will or should be like. On the basis of their own faint recollections of childhood, on reports solicited from children's older siblings, and on current cultural stereotypes about the richness of imagination and fantasy in young children, parents will suggest to children the sorts of things they are likely to dream.

In the earlier of the two studies (Foulkes, 1982a) described here, parents generally were absent or did not participate when their children prepared to go to bed. In the later project (Foulkes, Hollifield, Sullivan, Bradley, & Terry, 1990), however, because of changes in federal regulation on behalf of research subjects, especially children, parents played a much larger role in the immediate presleep period. Thus I was able directly to observe parental suggestion-planting about subsequent dream experiences. To be sure, not every parent did this, but the temptation to anticipate dream content and to review previously reported dreams by the children themselves or their siblings was evidently substantial. Of course, I had warned parents against making such suggestions, saying, essentially, let's just see what happens on its own, and I always had the last word before the sleep period began, reiterating that message to the child. But the presleep period often was rich in dream suggestions—topics, characters, and so on.

Why would parents make such suggestions, both in the immediate presleep period in a research project and more generally in their interaction with their children? Probably because of their belief in cultural stereotypes about the richness of children's imagination, and their not unnatural desire that their children prove to share such talent, and, in a research project, be able to manifest it to others. Back in the 1960s, when I began my research on children's dreams in a bucolic college town in the Rocky Mountain West, I could still be somewhat convincing when I explained (truthfully) to parents that the project wasn't a "test," that no one in fact knew what it meant to dream or not to dream, to remember a dream or not to remember a dream. Even then, some parental strivers pushed their children to "perform." On delivering the child home to her doorstep, for instance, I would be asked by a parent just roused from sleep, "Well, has she had a dream yet?" By the 1980s, in the urban center in which the second major study was conducted, that sort of attitude was much more widespread. Dreaming itself was "good," and having fanciful dreams especially so.

Now the concern with parental suggestions is not that they in fact have the power to create or modify dream *experiences* themselves. Adult dreams are largely resistant to voluntary or indirectly suggested presleep control, and in our research we have found the same to be true for children (Foulkes, Pivik, Steadman, Spear, & Symonds, 1967; Foulkes, 1982a). The major problem is in the telling: that when the child begins to recount the dream to the same person who has suggested what dreams are likely to be about, the dream *report* will, voluntarily or not, be shaped in the direction of those prior expectations. Since parents, naturally and almost inevitably, if often without realizing it, are the sources of these expectations, they generally make poor collectors of their own children's dreams. This is not to say that the expectation effect is absent with other interviewers, but at least it is not subject to powerful reinforcement.

Given this background, you will understand that I am not persuaded of "unbiased" parental interviewing even if I can read a transcript of a seemingly unbiased parent-child dream interview. It is not just what happens in that interview itself that is important: I also want to know how, preceding the interview and in the child's life more generally, the parent has characterized the act of dreaming.

Consider, for example, the conditions of a study (Resnick, Stickgold, Rittenhouse, & Hobson, 1994) conducted on the false assumption that I had no home-dream control reports for children in my longitudinal laboratory-dream study (Foulkes, 1996b). In this home-only study, professional parents from the Boston/Cape Cod area were asked to interview their children in the morning. In line with federal regulations, the parents presumably were told the purpose of the study, which was to challenge my own findings on the meagerness of young children's dreams. One can imagine, then, not only the general cultural pressure that contemporary Cambridge-area doctors and lawyers would feel to see to it that their children perform "well" in any test of imaginativeness, but also specific pressure from an investigative team whose theory (Hobson, 1988) also specifies that children's dream reports must be imaginative.

The parents' morning dream interviews were tape-recorded, providing some degree of protection against glaring bias in parental interviewing. But no recording was made of the presleep period, in which parents would be structuring the task for their children, and no independent observer was present during this period to control for parental pressure. Nor was any systematic observation made of other child-parent interactions on the topic of dreams and dreaming. On five of the study nights, children were told, according to the investigative team's own instructions, to repeat "I will remember my dreams" three times out loud just before going to sleep. Imagine that you are a child in this study. When mommy and daddy wake you up, or when you wake up on your own and then signal to them, do you want to have a dream to tell, a nice dream, the kind you know good and smart children can have? I think that, other things being equal, you do—even if you're not quite sure that there really was one there quite like the one that you now are telling.

I also do not recommend teacher-collected samples of children's dreams, for reasons having to do with when and where dreams should be collected. In earlier times, however, when dream collection was, in effect, a recess project, unconnected with the school curriculum, teacher participation was perhaps less objectionable than it is today, when the curriculum may well specify that dreaming is good and that dreams are an avenue to personal growth. The possibilities of suggestion on dream reporting here are immense, as they also are in comparable camp, workshop, or "group" situations.

So, *who* remains as a potentially good collector of children's dreams? Not surprisingly, perhaps, I plump for someone like myself, particularly in my role in the longitudinal study, in the course of which I got to know children over a five-year period in a well-defined research context (Foulkes, 1982a). I had no history of prior discourse with the children regarding dreaming, and in my research role sought continuously to avoid suggesting to children that it was good to dream or to dream certain kinds of dreams. I was dream-questioner, pure and simple, with no therapeutic purpose or any agenda other than meeting the requirements of an explicit research design. Over time, of course, relationships with the children developed, and we learned to know one another better and better. But even at the outset, the research plan created an environment of interpersonal trust and neutrality that would be difficult, if not impossible, to achieve in more casual and haphazard everyday encounters with children. This is the valuable other side of the coin of the "sterility" with which experimental situations in psychological research are so easily castigated.

It bears noting, moreover, that some of the frequently raised reservations about "neutral" interrogators are not generally well supported and in fact scarcely apply at all to children. Don't we often tell intimacies to strangers we meet by chance? Knowing how revealing they are alleged to be, are we especially reluctant to share our dreams with others? Not in my experience or that of other students of dreaming, particularly when it comes to cocktail or dinner parties. And children, in fact, make wonderful subjects in dream research precisely because they are not yet part of a culture which believes in the revealingness of dreaming—much better subjects than college sophomores whose heads are full of Freudian or Jungian theory. Whether, as at very young ages, they think that their dreams in some sense really happened, or at older ages, when they recognize that dreams are imaginings of the mind, children, in my substantial experience, treat their laboratory-reported dreams very matter-of-factly: such-and-such was my dream, no big deal.

The question whether children's dream reports are to be believed ultimately cannot be answered, because we don't have independent access to the dream experience (if any). We have nothing to compare the report to. This is also true for adults, though there the question of veracity doesn't bother us so much. But we do worry about children's dream reports because we suspect that children are more likely to tell us things for the effect they have on us, things that engage our attention or amuse us. I can still recall a conversation I had with a child many years ago which began with her alleged account of a dream. Whatever basis the "report" originally might have had in a real dream experience, it soon was quite evident that the purpose of her narrative was not any kind of reporting at all, but rather one of amusing me with an extravagant fantasy that I could almost literally see growing larger and more phantasmagoric minute by minute as I listened to it.

Once again, it must be stressed that there's no absolute way to verify dream reports, whether those of children or of adults. But my experience with children may entitle me to hazard a guess about one signpost to their dream reports' veracity. When dreams are told to me matter-of-factly (as they generally are on REM-sleep awakenings in the laboratory), I tend to believe. When they are told to me with an eye to making me collaborate in the dream or with the dreamer, when for instance the child is smiling at the apparent contemplation of the dream and thereby trying in a rather obvious way to get me to be amused by it too, then, as in the case of the girl just mentioned, I tend to doubt. I can't be sure in either case that I'm right, but I think the criteria I'm using are not unreasonable.

The *how* question about collecting children's dreams reports can be answered in terms of the preceding analysis. Children's dream reports should be solicited in a way that is structured along the lines of public opinion surveys, that is, with standard questions and with a humanly interested but impartial attitude in the interviewer. As in well-designed opinion surveys, the interviewer is given some latitude in phrasing unbiased follow-ups and in bridging topics. The interview is more than just reading a set list of questions; it is an information-gathering human interaction (Kahn & Cannell, 1957). But it is a human interaction within definite boundaries set by our knowledge of how both children and adults modify responses to meet perceived demand characteristics in an interview situation.

When should such interviews take place? Ideally, as soon as possible after the experience being reported has occurred. Just as you would rather trust the notes you made right after observing an automobile accident than your free recall of that accident hours or days later, you would be right to trust best the dream report that most immediately followed the dream. Sleep laboratory research has shown that there are systematic differences in dream reports made during the night on REM-sleep awakenings and later accounts of the same dreams given the following morning (see Foulkes, 1979).

Now some people would argue that the later reports in each case might be superior, that there is such a thing as delayed factual reminiscence (Montangero, Pasche, & Willequet, 1996). Sometimes that may be the case. Research on human memory suggests, however, that the far more common rule in delayed recall is selective forgetting and the assimilation of a particular event (or dream) to general assumptions about events (or dreams). Thus, as has been demonstrated for children's dream recall (Foulkes, 1979), if you reported a chase scene in your immediate recall of a dream but insisted that you were not anxious, by the time of your later morning recall it may seem plausible that, since there was a chase, you must have been anxious. Isn't that typically the case, you implicitly ask yourself, and shouldn't it have been true here?

But it's not just the protection of memory from later loss or distortion that argues for on-the-spot awakenings and reporting. As you may suspect, the social skills required to perform in the manner of the girl of the anecdote above are in relative abeyance on middle-of-the-night arousals. Just giving the facts, and that as sparsely as the interviewer permits, is chore enough in an intercom interview from a bed in a darkened laboratory room in the middle of the night. Finally, given the fact that you have just been awakened from REM sleep, during which the chance of having a dream is at its maximum, if you tell a dream, isn't it easier simply to report it while it is still fresh in your mind, rather than to have to make up something else from scratch?

It must be clear now *where* my argument is leading to: the sleep laboratory, which is, at present, the place where REM sleep is most reliably detected and impartial interviewing is most feasibly implemented. This may not always be the case; attempts are being made to develop at least semi-reliable

REM detectors for home use. The interviewer problem may, paradoxically, be the more difficult to solve: for comparison of persons and for generalized results, interviewing should be standardized, but that is very difficult to achieve if each dreamer interviews herself or himself. Then you have as many different interviewers as you have dreamers, probably none of them trained in the art and science of information-gathering.

The idea of using a laboratory to study psychological phenomena will seem appalling to some and arbitrary and unreasonable to others. Even some psychologists themselves eschew the laboratory and prefer more naturalistic methods of observation and philosophizing. But the more obvious ways of studying something like dreaming are full of flaws. It was not for no reason at all that laboratory research designs were first developed; it was because progress in understanding human experience required them. And, although much undoubtedly remains to be learned in psychology, the discipline can be proud of its achievements, particularly in the past half-century.

This certainly is the case in dream psychology since the discovery of REM sleep. Many questions that were totally up in the air in 1950 have since then been answered (see Foulkes, 1966) such as how long do dreams last? does everybody dream? how many dreams or how much dreaming do we do? These answers were achieved through laboratory studies of REM sleep dream reports (Foulkes, 1996a). In this light, casual dismissal of the laboratory method of dream study betrays ignorance of its considerable achievements.

It is thanks also to laboratory dream research that a major new insight into dream life during this century was achieved:

contrary to literary theory and to psychoanalysis, researchers found that nocturnal dreaming is a well-organized and generally realistic simulation of waking experience. With this observation, derived from representative samples of REM dreams from both adults and children (Snyder, 1970; Dorus, Dorus, & Rechtschaffen, 1971; Foulkes, Pivik, Steadman, Spear, & Symonds, 1967; Foulkes, 1982a; Foulkes & Schmidt, 1983), the entire premise of most earlier dream theories collapses. If dreams are typically both organized and mundane, then we don't have to create dream theories that are radically different from theories of waking thought. As the phenomena are continuous, so too must be the theories. Thus laboratory study has given us not only major new findings, but an altogether new slant on what dreaming is and on what a good dream theory should explain.

Yet however successful laboratory methods may have been elsewhere, their use with children still raises objections. Wouldn't children be terribly frightened, sleeping away from home and family? Wouldn't their dreams be so heavily influenced by the strangeness of the laboratory environment that any putative advantage of the representative sampling of REM sleep dreams would be vitiated by the unrepresentative content of these dreams?

These questions have occasioned concern not only from parents, but also from a number of my colleagues who have not studied children in the laboratory (Hunt, 1989; Resnick, Stickgold, Rittenhouse, & Hobson, 1994; Van de Castle, 1994). These critics, however, have ignored empirical data indicating that laboratory methods in dream research work out at least as well with children as with adults.

For instance, from presleep behavior ratings of the children in the longitudinal study (Foulkes, 1982a), we know that most often most of the children were judged to be moderately or extremely relaxed in the presleep period in the laboratory, and that extreme anxiety was very rare, even at the youngest ages at which children were studied (3 and 4). On only one of the 1,347 subject-nights in this study did the session have to be terminated because of a child's psychological distress. This child, then age 4, later became so comfortable in the laboratory that she was deliberately scheduled together with newly added children in subsequent years of the study to serve as a model of relaxed and competent participation. She simply had had, at age 4, a "bad" night, which, as any parent knows, can occur at home as well as away from home.

Most remarkably, *all* of the 14 children who entered the study at ages 3 and 4 remained in the study until its end 5 years later, each child serving a median of 9 laboratory nights per year. Physiological recordings taken in the laboratory confirmed that children slept well there, and that it was relatively easy for them to both fall asleep and stay asleep. Our children were by no means scared or unhappy during their periodic visits to the laboratory.

Whatever one's expectations might be about how children might react to having their sleep and dreams monitored in a sleep laboratory, the way they did in fact react in the longitudinal study suggests that their adaptation to the laboratory was at least as good as that of college students or adults. But what about their dreams? Surely, the objection is raised, they were influenced in a major way—distorted, in comparison to typical home dreams—by the laboratory environment, the presence of the experimenter/interviewer, the presence on most other nights of at least one other child, the fact of wearing electrodes on the face and scalp so that brainwaves and eye movements might be recorded, and so on. Once again, the data refute these seemingly reasonable but quite erroneous expectations.

Comparing home dreams with laboratory dreams is tricky because the laboratory *is* different from the home, not only in the respects just enumerated—the environment, the people, the apparatus—but also in the sampling plan used in collecting dreams. In the laboratory, a person typically is awakened several times during REM sleep episodes throughout the night, and is systematically questioned by an interviewer about the content of any remembered dreams. At home, a person wakes up on his or her own, sometimes during the night, but most typically only at the end of the night, and rehearses any remembered dreams in an unsystematic way. Given these differences in methods alone, one might expect differences between typically remembered home dreams and typically reported laboratory dreams. Such differences have been found with adults (see Domhoff, 1969), and we were able to replicate them with children (Foulkes, 1979). Our children, for instance, had more unpleasant dreams at home.

But there is good reason to believe that this finding reflects the method of dream sampling, and is not an effect of where—home versus laboratory—that method was used. The prevailing stereotypes of dreams as unpleasant and bizarre experiences depend on the kind of dream most likely spontaneously to catch our attention and to be processed for later recall when we are on our own. The dreams we notice and remember are the scary ones and the odd ones. Our blander and more realistic dreams cannot sustain more than passing notice, and, in fact, we sleep through most of them, never exposing their content to waking attention. So, on our own, we typically remember not only very few of our many REM dreams but also a very biased sample of the whole. It is only the representative sampling plan used in the laboratory that is capable of showing us the rest, and the bulk, of our dream life. This is precisely how the laboratory has altered our very conception of what dreams typically are like.

Still, the question remains, at what *cost* do we use laboratory methods? In view of the finding of more unpleasantness in home dreams in both children and adults, for example, some have argued that the laboratory makes people wary, that it inhibits the usual richness of our dream expression (see Domhoff, 1969 [who, however, no longer holds this view—Domhoff, 1996], and Hunt, 1989). Consequently, the mundaneness of laboratory dream reports is seen not as a new insight into the nature of dreams but as a situational "repression" (Hunt, 1989) induced by the laboratory situation—the place, the people, and the apparatus.

The best way to show that this is not the case, and that home dreams only seem to be different from laboratory dreams because they are sampled less adequately, would be to show that when dreams are sampled the same way in the home and the laboratory, there are no systematic differences between the two sets. This typically has been done by allowing persons to sleep until a set clock time, then wake them up and have them report their dreams (tape-record them, write them out, tell them to somebody). At home, this is done in the sleeper's usual environment, with the usual people around, and no unusual apparatus. In the laboratory, this is done away from home and family, with the experimenter present, and with electrode attachments and night-long recording of brainwaves and eye movements. The laboratory thus retains those features that are suspected of altering or taming typical dream life.

With adults, the result of such a method-controlled site comparison indicates little difference in dream content that is attributable to home versus laboratory as such (Weisz & Foulkes, 1970). In studies of the children in our longitudinal project, the results even more strongly suggest that there is no difference in dream content that is attributable to the "uniqueness" of the laboratory situation (Foulkes, 1979) When children's dreams are collected the same way at home and in the laboratory, neither the rate of dream recall nor the nature of dream content differ as a function of the setting. It is specifically interesting to note that, among 5- and 6-year-olds, this is true when dreams are told to the experimenter/interviewer in the laboratory and to a parent at home, when each is following the same interview procedures. Since we did find home versus laboratory dream differences when the method of dream collection was not the same in the two settings, the failure to find differences when the method was the same could not have resulted from some general insensitivity of our methods of dream analysis.

Clearly, the results of controlled comparisons of home versus laboratory dream sampling indicate that the sampling-plan advantage of the laboratory is not purchased at the cost of any systematic artifacts in dreams collected there. This conclusion is even better documented for children, specifically for the children in our longitudinal project, than it is for adults. And so, despite the many *a priori* reservations one might have had about bringing children to the laboratory to study their dream life, a substantial body of empirical evidence indicates that there are no grounds for such reservations.

But this evidence has not generally been accepted, and we need to ask why not. The very structure of this book provides the most important clue (and explains why its author didn't simply *start* by presenting his dream findings). When people have strong expectations about a phenomenon, and when a new method generates data contradicting those expectations, the natural human tendency is to find fault with the method, even when, as in this case, the empirical data show that the method of laboratory dream collection *cannot* be held to blame for the discrepancy.

But prior expectation is difficult to relinquish, and in the still scientifically primitive field of dream psychology, it has proved to be especially persistent. There are those who want to disbelieve, either on theoretical grounds (Hunt, 1989; Resnick, Stickgold, Rittenhouse, and Hobson, 1994) or on methodological ones (Van de Castle, 1994), the validity of laboratory dream research with children, despite the extensive data I have collected showing an absence of laboratory-induced effects on children's dreaming.

One popular book widely disseminated by a general book club takes a position in support of the commonplace apprehensions about children-in-the-laboratory without ever mentioning the home-versus-laboratory evidence collected from the children in my longitudinal study—evidence that contradicts precisely these apprehensions (Van de Castle, 1994). Given this climate of evaluation, it seemed important to establish, in advance of my data presentation, that there is *no* valid empirical reason why children's dream life should not be studied systematically with the very best methods available and those that have proved so valuable with adults—namely, REM sleep awakenings in the laboratory.

Are Sleep-Laboratory Dreams "Real" Dreams?

A few readers of the foregoing section remain unconvinced by my argument in favor of sleep-laboratory dream research with children. They have argued that other ways of studying dreams are appropriate to research objectives other than my own, and that the very failure of laboratory research to support common assumptions about children's and adult's dreams must indicate some shortcoming in laboratory dream data. In effect, the "real" dream is the one we know in everyday life, and methods therefore are required (such as adults' dream diaries, or collections of dreams that children have recounted to parents at the breakfast table) that will both address and validate this everyday reality.

I am reluctant to approach the slippery slope of what is real and what not, or of what is "more" real and "less" real, among dream phenomena. I do think, however, that these objections to the primacy and/or validity of sleep-laboratory dream methods (which you, the reader, may well share) are deserving of some response.

My dictionary (the third edition of *The American Heritage Dictionary of the English Language*) gives the following first definition of "dream": "A series of images, ideas, emotions, and sensations occurring involuntarily in the mind during certain stages of sleep." (Other definitions follow, such as "trance," "wild fancy or hope," which are not germane to the discussion here.) The quasi-geographical notion of a dream's location ("in the mind") is certainly fuzzy, but may mean to point to the dream's being consciously experienced. It is interesting to note that the definition does seem to have been influenced by laboratory research ("during certain stages . . ."), even if not in an altogether accurate way.

But our ideas about the sorts of mental activity we experience during sleep (and certain waking states) have changed since the advent of modern sleep-and-dream research. We have learned that what we describe, on being awakened immediately following our involuntary mental experiences during sleep, does not always agree very well with our everyday memories or concepts of dream experiences. We have, as it were, dreams-on-the-spot and dreams-at-some-reflective-distance. At least this is how dream researchers often have viewed the matter, pointing, as have I, to the inherent loss and alteration of dream material as time goes by and as memory works its way through and around that material.

It now seems, however, that this formulation may not go far enough. Thanks to laboratory research, we can see that there are at least *two realities* in the dream world. I now make so bold as to define them. Dream A is the involuntary conscious experience of mentation during sleep and some other states, most often in the form of momentary, and, if sequential, narrative, imagery. Our best, and perhaps only reliable, knowledge of this mentation comes from a person's report recorded immediately following abrupt arousal from the experience in question. The prime instance of Dream A is, of course, the laboratory dream report. It best fits the dictionary sense of conscious experiences "occurring . . . during . . . sleep," but the nature and properties of these experiences were largely misunderstood until the discovery of REM sleep.

Dream B is a person's everyday account of an experience, described with greater or lesser accuracy and with greater or lesser conviction, as having occurred during sleep. The forms of Dream B are far more varied than those of Dream A, because they are much more responsive to the diverse waking personal and social situations of the dreamer. Dreams of class B are likely to be imbued with value, and to be viewed by the dreamer as being emblematic of the self and of the dreamer's current personal situation and development. These dreams are embedded, at least when rehearsed or recounted, in the person's notion of selfhood. They are important "personal" property.

As shared with others, in psychotherapy or other more or less ritualized social encounters, these dreams also are social currency. They are shaped by the dream-teller's expectations of the listeners' reactions, and by those reactions themselves. In both its intrapersonal and interpersonal contexts, Dream B often attains the status of a relatively benign form of "false consciousness" (Hacking, 1995), a historically false but personally significant memory (Spanos, 1996). I suspect, for instance, that more than a few of the published dreams of Carl Jung (see 1965) are dreams in the sense of B, rather than conscious experiences that, as such, ever actually occurred during any stage of sleep.

More generally, although once thought to index Dream A, Dream B is now best conceived as a waking personal/social construct that often has minimal, and sometimes no, relation to involuntary sleep mentation. This does not mean, however, that Dream B is not "real": it has the same status for the personalistic and social disciplines as any other value-impregnated belief. But it does mean that the dictionary needs another, more value-imbued meaning for what has been posing for all these years as Dream A.

In the distinction between Dreams A and B, one sees not only two kinds of dream phenomena, but also the two worlds of dream discourse. The direct, phenomenological observations of the sleep laboratory are important both to the process-psychologist who wants to know "how the mind works" during sleep and to the biological scientist who wants to know the ongoing mental correlates of biologically recorded events during sleep. From another perspective, the more personalistic and social disciplines study the dream as potentially symbolic of personal needs and values and of social statuses, functions, and dysfunctions. And many persons who identify themselves as "dream psychologists" (Van de Castle, 1994) seem much less interested in how the mind works during sleep than in the personal and social values attaching to Dream B. The disjunction between these two worlds of dream discourse helps to explain how it is that, although psychoanalysis and its dream theory have been thoroughly discredited in the biological and cognitive sciences, they can still live on, and even reign, in "symbolic" or content-based disciplines such as literature, the arts, and in content-centered areas of "dream psychology."

The evident displeasure of people in these fields with the results (and therefore the methods) of laboratory dream research is intended as a reproach of laboratory dream research.

The same holds true for the unhappiness of individuals whose impressions of their own or of their children's dreams are so much at apparent odds with laboratory dream data. But the reproach, I'm afraid, may lie in the other direction. We had been led to believe that Dream B was the same as Dream A, and that its peculiarities and its symbolism simply reflected unique properties of the sleeping/dreaming mind. Now we see, with much better evidence, that this is not the case. Therefore, the nature and language and functions of those waking myths that pose as simple products of sleeping mental processes no longer can be traced to those processes. The study of Dream B, that is, has been shaken loose from its supposed foundations in the psychology of the "unconscious" dreaming mind proposed by Freud in his major contribution, *The Interpretation of Dreams* (1900), in which children always dream of simple wish-fulfillments and adults of conflicted impulses undergoing repression.

The results of modern dream research have not only inadvertently identified a new definition or class of "dream," one largely detached from the dictionary sense of involuntary thought processes of the sleeping mind, but they have also removed what heretofore were the evidential foundations for most content-oriented approaches to this sort of dream. In one sense, this is good news for, say, the anthropologist concerned with the personal and cultural uses of dream narratives. It means that her or his current methods—collecting dream reports in casual conversation, observing dream-related rituals, and so on—are entirely adequate and appropriate to the task at hand, which is to explain the personal and cultural roles and meanings of dreams of class B. Nothing would be gained, and much lost, if the collection of dream observations were made in some makeshift "sleep laboratory" at the edge of the settlement.

The bad news, however, is that much theoretical rethinking is in order. Whatever role Dream B phenomena may play for individuals, or for a society as a whole, that role is not going to be best formulated in terms of any theory that purports to describe the workings of the sleeping mind. The waking myth is not like Dream A, and it can't be explained in terms of observation of dreams as they actually are experienced.

So, yes, there are different objectives and methods in the study of dreams, particularly depending on whether you mean Dream A or Dream B. And it ought not to be surprising that the child's mentation report (or absence of such) in the laboratory, told emotionlessly to a neutral interviewer, will differ from the engaging Dream B told to an obviously interested parental audience around the breakfast table. Students of dreams must decide whether they wish to study the maturation of the child's sleeping mind and brain, or her/his socialization into the world of waking symbolic life. The focus of my research, and of this book, is upon how the child's mind "works" during sleep, and upon how the workings of that mind grow and develop throughout childhood.

3

The Two Studies

The results of this book rest on my two major studies, one longitudinal and one cross-sectional. Longitudinally, one would compare mental abilities at ages 5 and 7 by restudying, at age 7, children already studied two years earlier at age 5. Cross-sectionally, one might compare mental abilities at ages 5 and 7 by studying, during the same year, kindergartners and second-graders from the same school. Although more time-consuming and costly, and therefore much less frequently done, longitudinal studies obviously are better geared to the detection of fine-scale changes in mental or behavioral development.

The larger of the two studies (Foulkes, 1982a) was longitudinal. It was, in fact, the most extensive sleep-laboratory project ever conducted on the dreams of either children or adults. It began in 1968 and continued into 1973. Although the wave of research funding already had crested by 1968, this project managed to obtain federal support. The second, cross-sectional project (Foulkes, Hollifield, Sullivan, Bradley, & Terry, 1990) was initiated in the mid 1980s, with limited funding from the State of Georgia. Research funds now seem to be allocated in different areas, however, and it is not likely that there will soon be follow-up research to elaborate upon or to modify the results described here for very young children. (Inge Strauch and colleagues in Switzerland have done important studies with older children comparable in age to those I studied; see Strauch & Meier, 1996.) Hence, although one may wish that some things had been done differently in one or both studies, we have, perforce, to accept them as they are, as both our best and in many instances our only source of information on what children's dream life and dreaming capacity seem to be like when they are investigated with the best and the only adequate technology available for their systematic study.

The first, longitudinal study became so big and wide-ranging in part because so little was known about the subject. Since we literally didn't know where to begin in approaching children's dreams, we began everywhere. In our program of daytime testing, for instance, we threw in every kind of observation we could think of, from physical maturation to personality to play behavior to family life to cognitive development. Fortunately, by the time of the second, cross-sectional study, a pattern had emerged from the first, so that the far scantier resources then available could be harnessed to a far more modest research design that sought to cross-validate the earlier pattern.

The Longitudinal Study

We advertised for subjects in the daily newspaper of Laramie, Wyoming, the *Daily Boomerang,* named for the mule of its first editor, the humorist Bill Nye. Because of the duration of the

Table 1. The longitudinal study

| Group | Number of children by study year | | |
	Year 1	Year 3	Year 5
Younger	7F and 7M; ages 3–5	7F and 7M; now ages 5–7	7F and 7M; now ages 7–9, *plus* 7F, newly inducted, ages 7–9
Older	8F and 8M; ages 9–11	8F and 6M (2 dropouts); now ages 11–13, *plus* 6M, newly inducted, ages 11–13	7F (1 dropout) and 11M (1 dropout); now ages 13–15

project, we requested volunteers whose parents were permanent residents (rather than, for instance, students just passing through town). We asked for volunteers at the starting ages of 3 and 4, and 9 and 10. The volunteers we did accept, and who accepted us, ranged from 2 years 9 months to 4 years 8 months in the younger group (14 children, 7 boys and 7 girls), and from 8 years 8 months to 11 years 9 months in the older group (16 children, 8 boys and 8 girls). Only 3 children in the younger group had not yet reached their third birthday and only 1 child in the older group had passed his eleventh birthday (ages are at the onset of the study, June 1, 1968).

As one may imagine, the motives for volunteering were somewhat different in the two age groups. While parents took the initiative in volunteering younger children, with the evident belief that service in the study would be intellectually and emotionally enriching for their children, older children often took the initiative in volunteering, evidently swayed by our financial incentives. We had promised that children who completed service in the 5-year project could earn as much as $500, half of it along the way, half upon completion. While this incentive system no doubt played some role in keeping the children in the study (all 14 younger children stayed in the study for all 5 years, as did 12 of 16 children in the older group, the exceptions being children whose families moved out of town), I don't think it was decisive. That is, I don't think children would have remained, or parents would have let them remain, if we hadn't also made their laboratory experience pleasant and interesting.

The idea behind running the two age groups at the same time was that, in 5 years of study time, we could collect data on the development of dreaming from age 3 (start of the first year for the youngest children) to age 15 (end of the last year for the oldest children). Moreover, by comparing younger children at the end of their series with older children at the beginning of their series, we could check to see whether children's results were being affected by repeated service in the study itself.

As a further test of this possibility, we added six 11- and 12-year-old boys in the third year of the study (for comparison with the 6 boys remaining from the original group) and seven 7- and 8-year-old girls in the fifth year of the study (for comparison with the 7 girls of the original group). In each case, the data suggested that repeated laboratory testing had little systematic effect on children's dreams, an issue which always is a concern in longitudinal research. (In his critique, Van de Castle [1994] mistakes both the rationale for and the nature of this check on the effects of repeated testing: "Additional subjects had to be added to replace children who dropped out"; p. 315.)

Altogether, 43 children served in the project for one year, 34 for three years, and 26 (of the original 30 inductees) for all five years. In the design of the study, the major years for developmental dream comparisons were the first, third, and fifth years (from here on, I will refer to these years as the "normative-data" years). In these years, all children in both age groups were studied identically: 9 nights of laboratory service, spaced through the year, with 3 awakenings scheduled each night, predominantly, but not always, from REM sleep. On the second and ninth nights of each of these years, I tried systematically to "influence" children's dreams by either rubbing their faces with a soft cotton puff, moving an exposed limb, or using a light spray of water. As is also true for adults, such influence was only infrequently observed, suggesting that children don't rely more on external stimulation than do adults in composing their dreams.

On each laboratory night, seven small metal disks, approximately the diameter of a pencil, were affixed to the face and scalp of the child so that continuous night-long recordings might be taken of the child's brainwaves (EEG) and eye movements. These recordings allowed us to determine whether the child was awake or asleep, and, if asleep, whether in REM sleep or non-REM sleep. Awakenings for dream retrieval were made on the basis of these recordings. Electrode disks were affixed by tape or other means, and connection between the disks and the recording equipment was effected by tiny wires leading from the disk to a terminal box at the head of the bed, and thence by cable to an electroencephalograph in our "control" room, adjacent to the child's bedroom.

On reading this, you may well put yourself among the many critics of the sleep laboratory as an investigative site in the study of dreaming. But as anyone who has actually slept in such a laboratory can attest, you rapidly become quite unaware of the electrodes and their wires. There is plenty of play in the wires, so there is no problem in changing position or tossing and turning. Since the EEG is a recording procedure, and not one of stimulation, nothing is "felt" during the session. As our sleep data showed, the children readily adapted to having the recordings taken. To the extent that children ever were upset or frightened in the laboratory, it had nothing to do with our procedures, but rather stemmed from the same aspects of the sleep situation that children find upsetting at home: social isolation and being in the dark.

Generally, two or three children were studied on a given night. Where there were natural preferences (brother and sister coming together) or where such preferences developed over the course of the project, we honored them. Sometimes, since the older and younger groups were being studied simultaneously, a younger child might already be asleep by the time an older one arrived at the laboratory. Children's arrival times were scheduled one half hour before their supposed bedtimes, but we gave children time to "wind down" before putting them off to bed in one of our bedrooms. Both the open area in which electrodes were attached and the bedrooms themselves were equipped with posters, books, and toys designed to appeal to the children, and children often were visibly excited by the prospect of coming to visit the laboratory.

I was in charge of taking the recordings, and of interviewing the children, on every laboratory night during the normative-data years. I generally worked alone, although other lab personnel or students sometimes were present for at least part of a night. Many parents would simply drop off their children, while some would stay until a younger child was in bed or asleep. When parents were not present, I defined my role in a relatively passive way, so that ratings of the children's presleep behavior that I made on each evening would not be contaminated by differences in my own behavior. At bedtime for the younger children, however, I often served as a parental surrogate, reading stories to them before lights out. Once children were abed, my role became that of a competent adult babysitter, meeting children's requests (for a drink, to go to the bathroom, and so on) and otherwise comforting them. Intercoms from each bedroom to the control area meant that, both before falling asleep and on spontaneous awakenings, children always could make their wishes known to me.

For the sake of variety, and to collect information on the generality of our normative-year data, the second and fourth years of the project were differently structured than the first, third, and fifth. It was then that we did our systematic home-versus-laboratory dream comparisons. We also evaluated the effect of certain other features of our normative-data year laboratory methods on children's dreams: by using a different interview, by using different interviewers, by using intercom versus in-room interviews, and by having commercial television available during the presleep period. We found no indication that our procedures were systematically biasing our normative-data year results.

Until ages 7 and 8, the younger children were interviewed at their bedside; later, they were interviewed just as the older children always had been, via an intercom from the control area. We suspected that very young children might not understand talking to "the wall." A standardized interview was used in each case, with a simplified form for younger children. Although the opening question, "What were you dreaming just before I woke you up?" might suggest that a dream was occurring at that time, children were told that it was not expected that they always would remember a dream, only that they always try to do so. Other than the initial question, the interview format was more relaxed than directive, my guess being that pressuring children might result in reports that had nothing to do with any actual dream. When children said that they could remember something, they were probed regarding characters, settings, activities, and feelings. At very young ages, when not all children showed a good grasp of the concept "dream," they might be asked questions that avoided this term, such as "What were you seeing?" or "What was happening just before I woke you up?"

To evaluate how well children understood what a dream is, we used a standardized test (Laurendeau & Pinard, 1962). Other tests, given specifically to help us evaluate children's dream data, included tests of waking memory, tests requiring that children describe pictorial stimuli either physically present or recently removed from view, and tests of language skills. The obvious intent here was to evaluate objections that our children's dream reports were misleading because the children didn't understand the interview questions, couldn't remember very well, or didn't have the ability accurately to describe events they had experienced.

I already noted that we collected a much wider variety of waking information from and about our children for comparison with their dream reports and dream reporting. Ideally, these data could tell us who, given his or her other personal characteristics, dreams certain kinds of dreams particularly often, or simply remembers dreams in general particularly often. Our most ambitious project was a nursery school that we ran for all the younger children for two weeks during each of their first three summers in the study. Here we systematically observed and recorded children's play behavior and their interaction with others and with teachers. Whether from such observation or from more standardized tests, the data we collected from or about children finally were described as rankings or scores that could be correlated statistically with scores or rankings on dream variables; in effect, a comparison of the daytime child with the nighttime child.

Generally, two or three waking test sessions were scheduled during each year of a child's service in the study. The monograph (Foulkes, 1982a) originally describing this research lists 657 nondream variables that we correlated with children's dream data, and notes that we computed, thanks to high-speed computers, some 136,411 such correlations. Obviously, with so many correlations, many might seem "significant" (in the statistical sense) simply by chance. But equally obviously, a study of the magnitude of our examination of children's REM sleep dreams was not likely soon to be repeated, so we wanted to include every waking observation that might even remotely be considered to have something to do with dreaming. The significance of any finding we made could be determined in subsequent, smaller-scale and more focused studies. That was, of course, part of the motivation of the second, cross-sectional study, which successfully replicated a pattern of relationships between waking mental abilities and children's dreams that we had found in the longitudinal study. The number of waking variables we collected for comparison with dreams gives one indication of the magnitude of the longitudinal study. Here's another: there were 1,347 child-nights in the laboratory, and during normative-data years 2,711 dream interviews were conducted there. I think that you will agree with me that it would have constituted criminal neglect to have collected so many dream data and not to have searched far and wide for waking variables related to them.

Getting the dream data into the form of numbers or scores has always seemed problematic to critics of dream research. Doubting that such reduction could be accomplished, such critics cast doubt on the very possibility of any meaningful scientific study of dreams. But in parallel to the accomplishment of being able to identify when during sleep particularly vivid dreaming might be happening (REM sleep), dream researchers also have made considerable progress in developing content-analysis systems (Domhoff, 1996) and rating scales (Winget & Kramer, 1979) describing dream reports. These procedures have served to identify major features of dream experience so that they might be counted and judged reliably, that is, comparably by different judges using the same rules.

On the basis of earlier work by others, we developed in the longitudinal study a comprehensive content-analysis and rating scheme for scoring children's dream reports. A manual prepared for use by our judges was itself a small book (Foulkes & Shepherd, 1971). The content analysis scored different classes of dream characters, settings, sensory and motor activities, cognitive and emotional states, body-state or interpersonal motives, and actor outcomes relative to interpersonal motives and intentions.

Following the content-analysis results, judges then gave the dreams ratings for their overall pleasantness versus unpleasantness, for the degree of active participation of the self character in dream events, for the degree of realism versus distortion in dream characterization and settings, and for the visual versus merely conceptual nature of dream experience. The realism/distortion ratings were attempts to determine the mundaneness versus bizarreness of the children's dreams (see the claim that we made "no explicit attempt . . . . to score children's dream reports for bizarreness" [Resnick, Stickgold, Rittenhouse, & Hobson, 1994, p. 31]). We demonstrated good reliability for our procedures of dream analysis, that is, our judges agreed well with one another on both the contents and the overall quality of children's dream reports.

The Cross-Sectional Study

I attempted to replicate a pattern of the longitudinal findings concerning dream development between the ages of 5 and 8 with a second sample of children from the metropolitan Atlanta area. In many respects, this "replication" seemed to take place on a different planet than the longitudinal study. Beginning in 1984 and continuing through the next three years, the cross-sectional study gathered its children much more slowly and much less surely. In the longitudinal study, almost every child whose parent phoned us following our initial newspaper advertisement eventually served in the laboratory. In the

Table 2. The cross-sectional study

| Age | Number of children studied, by age | | |
	Girls	Boys	Total
5	10	10	20
6	10	10	20
7	10	10	20
8	10	10	20
	—	—	—
	40	40	80

cross-sectional study, it took 232 completed phone interviews and considerably more advertising to meet an enrollment quota of 80 children, this despite the fact that the service requirements in Atlanta were so much less demanding (3 nonconsecutive nights of laboratory study) than those in Laramie.

In part, this difference in recruitment may simply reflect the difference between a trusting small-town environment and a wary urban one. But also, in intervening years, a trend in American society led toward much greater parental suspicion of professionals working with children, a development that was reflected in the increased federally mandated scrutiny of research with children. In our case, it now was required that we save one of our two bedrooms for possible use by an accompanying parent on each study night. This meant that children always had to be studied one at a time. And greater parental presence also carried with it a much greater risk of parental suggestion as to the child's laboratory performance.

Just by themselves these differences, which were wholly outside our control, would have made it impossible literally to recreate the circumstances in which the longitudinal data had been collected. But I already had decided, by selecting a cross-sectional design, not to attempt a literal replication of the earlier project. That decision carried risks, for if data patterns of the earlier study were not observed in the later one, that could be attributed to the different methods of the two studies, rather than to the basic unreliability of the data patterns themselves. On the other hand, if (as it in fact turned out) the data patterns could again be observed *despite* the difference in method (and in the social context in which the research was conducted), we would gain enhanced assurance that those patterns really do exist and are sufficiently robust to be observable in different methodological and social contexts.

Compared to its predecessor, the cross-sectional study was focused. First, our interest was restricted to REM dreams. Thus there were no non-REM awakenings, and only 10 REM awakenings spread over three nights of laboratory service. Laboratory recordings of brainwaves and eye movements were taken much as in the earlier study, although our earlier experience suggested that it was not necessary to glue electrodes over hairy areas of the scalp. Then, the study was limited to paid volunteers *ages 5 to 8,* because these were ages that the longitudinal study had suggested were associated with major changes in the amount and the form of dream experience in early childhood. Last, we focused on *cognitive* waking variables, since the longitudinal study had also suggested that certain classes of waking mental skill were critical to the unfolding of competence in dreaming.

To permit more precise determination of age-related changes in dream experience, we studied 20 children (10 boys and 10 girls), each within a month of his or her 5th, 6th, 7th, and 8th birthday. (This proved somewhat confusing to some parents, who wondered if we were studying the effect of birthdays on dreaming.) As in our earlier study, when it was not strictly required, we told parents of the children precisely what we were studying and why, as was now mandatory. But the change from before was that we now had a much better idea of what we expected to find, and thus had to tell parents our hypothesis, based on the data of the longitudinal study, that dream development reflected waking mental development. The greater pressure we observed parents exerting on children to "do well" may have been a result.

Our limited program (4 sessions) of cognitive testing focused on some variables that we thought, from the earlier study, might correlate well with dream development (measures of visual-spatial imagination, such as Wechsler Block Design, and a "mental rotation" experiment [Foulkes, Sullivan, Hollifield, & Bradley, 1989], both of which require children mentally to manipulate figures or figural patterns) as well as some variables whose role in dream development was not established in the earlier study and which we wished to rule out (measures of language proficiency).

Both dream interviews and dream analyses were focused on dimensions identified in the earlier study as particularly important ones in dream development. I was again the interviewer on all nights. Awakenings were by voice, at the child's bedside. If parents still were awake, they were permitted to listen to dream interviews over an intercom in the control area, but not to enter the child's bedroom at that time. I followed an interview schedule that presented children with several Yes-No questions to make it easy to scale the child's response on dimensions of interest: the presence of visual imagery ("Could you see what was happening?"), the static versus movielike quality of dream imagery ("Could you see [person, object, etc.] moving?"), self-participation in dream events ("Were you in this dream?" and, if so, "What were you doing?"), and narrative development. Immediately after each interview, I filled out rating scales, based on the child's responses to questions on these dream dimensions. These ratings later were verified (or changed) by a second judge. Reliable outside ratings of narrative development in dream reports also were obtained, with the low end of the scale representing discontinuous scenes and the higher end allotted to purposeful episodes, in which characters do things in order to achieve some particular outcome over time.

As in the longitudinal project, we were able to establish children's successful adaptation to the laboratory situation. Presleep behavior ratings indicated relaxation as the general rule, and children at all age levels typically fell asleep within 15 minutes of lights-out, and maintained sleep well.

Also as in the earlier study, waking test data were collected by colleagues who did not know the children's dream data, and I did not know the children's test scores when I interviewed them in the laboratory. I did know, or could readily guess just from talking with children, their approximate ages; it's difficult to mistake a 5-year old for an 8-year old. But we did not have the resources to bring in an interviewer blind to our earlier findings. Faced with the choice of proceeding in the face of this handicap or of doing nothing, I went ahead.

The following three chapters will summarize the findings of the longitudinal study and the cross-sectional replication at three different age groupings: 3 to 5 (longitudinal study only);

5 to 9 (both studies); and 9 to 15 (longitudinal study only). For the longitudinal study, the assignment of dream competencies to any particular age can be only approximate (that is, some "3 and 4-year olds" actually started the study at age 2, and one "9 and 10-year old" was 11 when his service began). Since the cross-sectional children were studied within a month of some particular birthday, their age norms are more meaningful. But the major point brought out by the data is that, particular ages aside, there are *stages* in dream development. The child doesn't always dream as often as or in the same way as we do. We humans become, over a particular course in childhood, more frequent and more fluent dreamers.

Although we studied both girls and boys, I am not going to be describing any sex differences, because I do not think our data indicate any important sex differences in the course of the development of dreaming competence. This is not to say that the *content* of boys' and girls' dreams is always interchangeable, any more than is the content of their daytime experiences. Rather, I'm suggesting that, when we focus on the *process* of dreaming rather than on dream content, sex-related differences do not seem to be important.

4

Ages Three to Five

Paucity of Dreams

The single most amazing finding of ours—the result of the best available method to study children's dreaming in the preschool years—was how puny the dream process turned out to be. However rich and detailed preschoolers' dream "reports" may be when they are elicited at some delay by parents, clinicians, or other credulous interviewers, when children are awakened during REM sleep periods and asked, on the spot, if and what they were dreaming, the most common response by far is that they were not dreaming anything at all.

The typical (median) preschool child in the longitudinal study reported dreams on only 15% of REM awakenings (and on 0% of non-REM awakenings). Moreover, the reports the children gave were very brief and insubstantial (a median of 13–14 words per report). Social interaction, which is the prime currency of the dream world in adult reports, was almost wholly lacking in the children's reports. Only very rarely was there a description of an active self character, that is, of a self who actively participates in dream events, which is another general characteristic of adults' dream reports. Only a quarter of the preschoolers' reports described any locomotion or generalized movement; their dreaming was more like a slide than a movie.

Credibility

But is this, you are no doubt asking yourself, what young children's dreams are *really* like? Isn't it more likely a picture of children's dream life that has been contaminated by their poor memory, lack of interest, or poor descriptive skills? Ultimately, of course, we can't be sure whether or how well the children's dream reports reflect dream experiences.

As with the dream reports of adults, however, we can devise a system of collection of children's dream reports that will increase our confidence about their accuracy. By collecting the reports in the laboratory, for instance, with crisp awakenings during periods of sleep in which we suspect the potential for dreaming is maximal, we have created a situation that enhances the prospects of accurate reporting. We are not at the mercy of persons just "happening" later to recall, with the possibility of much intervening loss or change of material, a dream that, unlike the many others subsequently lost to recall, has managed to attract the waking interest or attention of the dreamer. With rapid awakenings initiated by another person, we are not dependent on dreams that, in comparison to most others, just "happen" to wake the dreamer up, possibly in a slow and disoriented way that confuses the recall of dream events with the recall of ideas or feelings that were experienced during the process of waking up.

In a research setting, we also can systematically collect information on the characteristics or traits of the persons giving the reports. We used our testing program in both studies to find out which kinds of children were reporting dreams most often and which kinds of children were reporting particular kinds of dreams most often. One finding, or rather lack of a finding, that we made suggests that the major artifact in our preschoolers' dream reports might not be *under*reporting, but rather, *over*reporting. That is, spurred by parental expectation or other factors, some children might be telling dreams that in fact had not happened. The negative finding in question is the lack of correlation, within the group of 3- and 4-year-olds, between age and rate of dream reporting. In fact, the highest-rate reporters on REM sleep awakenings among girls (57%) and boys (73%) were the very youngest in the group. Why is this disturbing? Our findings across study years indicate that recall increases with age, a relationship that is, on many grounds, a plausible one. But the two highest-rate reporters at ages 3 and 4 later showed *decreases* in report rates, as if they now understood their role better and were reporting dreams both less frequently and more accurately.

Likewise casting some doubt on even the meager set of dreams that we did collect at ages 3 and 4 is the finding that they did not tend to come, as they did at later ages, from the smartest children. No cognitive-skill variable predicted rate of dream reporting at ages 3 and 4, and this includes ones that we had included especially because of their potential for verifying report credibility, such as children's understanding of what a dream is, their waking memory skills, and their waking accuracy in describing pictorial stimuli or events. Variables that *did* predict REM recall at ages 3 and 4 did so uniquely at that age, and suggested a pattern of dependence on adults, talkativeness, and spontaneity in verbal expression. Thus, rather than being competent dreamers or accurate reporters, our 3- and 4-year-old dreamers may have tended to be children with both the desire and the means of pleasing their adult interviewer.

Our findings do not therefore paint an altogether pretty picture of the dream-reporting abilities of 3- and 4-year-olds. But they do suggest that the larger problem in studying young children may be their motivation to tell dreams when dreams seem to be expected even if they weren't experienced, rather than insufficient motivation to report accurately. Even in the optimal conditions of the laboratory, confabulation in the service of pleasing or appeasing adults remains a problem in research with preschoolers. In fact, my belief that children's laboratory dream reports first become *generally* credible at age 5 or so explains why, in the cross-sectional follow-up, we did not try to study children at a younger age.

If you were to ask me, therefore, how certain I am about the discussion that follows about children's dreams and dreaming at ages 3 to 5, I would have to admit that I am less certain about it than about anything else in my data presentation. Indeed, I don't see how anybody could be very certain about the dream life of preschoolers, and I certainly don't see how one could be as certain as other writers and researchers (for example, Garfield, 1984), using much less satisfactory methods, seem to be. But my continuing the present discussion indicates that I do believe my findings with the preschoolers have some credibility.

One reason is that they are consistent with the findings of others on waking imagination and intelligence. Another is that the 3- and 4-year-olds in the longitudinal study showed the same psychophysiological discriminations in dream reporting as did presumably more credible adults, reporting dreams significantly more often on REM sleep awakenings than on non-REM awakenings, for instance, and reporting non-REM dreams more often from light than deep non-REM stages. Those findings suggest that the children's rate of dream reporting bears some relationship to their rate of dream experiencing. Finally, some of the distinctive positive features of the preschoolers' REM reports do seem to be quite credible.

Animals and Body States

Until now, most of what I've said about the children's dream reports has had to do with aspects of dreaming that we adults take for granted but that preschoolers seem *not* to experience: social interaction, movement, active self-participation. If children don't have these dream features, what *do* they dream?

Two features stood out in our sample of preschoolers' dreams: animal characters and body-state references. An animal dream report might be something like the following: a bird singing; a calf in its barn; chickens eating corn. Note that, in line with the list of negative dream features above, such reports do not have a narrative quality, they don't involve social interaction or character locomotion, and they don't mention the dreamer as a participating dream character.

The body-state theme implied motives relating to a dream character's own body rather than to other actors in a social world. Interestingly enough, sleep rather than hunger was their more frequent concern, whereas the reverse was true for adults and also in later childhood. And, while hunger primarily motivated other dream characters, such as the chickens eating their corn, fatigue or sleep states were almost always ascribed to the self character: I'm asleep in a barber shop; I'm asleep in an unfamiliar house; I'm asleep in a bathtub.

It is important to note that, although both animal characterization and body-state themes were found, at reduced levels, at later ages, it was only in the preschool years that we found animal characters relatively more dominant than human characters, and body-state themes relatively more dominant than social-interaction themes. That is, two years later, the dreams of these same children did not show the unique positive features found in the dreams they reported as preschoolers.

Although the prevalence of animal over human characters has also been noted in research using other methods of dream collection, it remains somewhat suspicious. Children generally have much more experience with other humans than with animals. Why all this animal dreaming? Is this part of children's confabulatory response to the implied demand, when asked about dreams, to tell a "story"? We adults express our notion of story to children largely with animal examples, whether through the medium of fairy tales, cartoon animals, or our barnyard "friends."

Psychologists have long speculated about the evident fascination animals have for children (see Foulkes, 1982a, pp. 48–49). Is it because they move fast or behave impulsively? Do we adults help to create this fascination through our cautionary fairy tales involving animals, or are we simply appealing to a fascination that's already there? Or maybe children don't discriminate between humans and other animals the way we do, seeing instead the animal kingdom as one big inclusive family?

These are questions that can't really be answered. But we do know some facts about children and animals. We know that, when children are asked to make up stories, these stories, particularly in the preschool years, have dominantly animal characters (Pitcher & Prelinger, 1963). We know that the identification of the storyteller with the animal character is such that the animal may, at some point in the story, become the child *(ibid.)*. We know that animals in children's stories are not selected simply for their familiarity; it's not the case that their stories revolve around their own pets, for example. And in the preschoolers' REM dreams, the most frequently appearing animals came from the same menagerie found in fairy tales, cartoons, and children's stories: neither highly familiar pets such as dogs and cats nor highly exotic animals such as polar bears or giraffes. Children's dream life thus seems to be similar to their waking imagination and narration, in the sense that animals can carry human concerns and readily become objects of identification.

But maybe this is because what we are taking as the children's dream life is really just another instance of making up a waking story, in this case when someone asks about a remembered dream. Is there any evidence to support the contention that the preschoolers' reports of animal dreaming were credible reports of actual dream experience? We did find that preschoolers who reported animal characters to the relative exclusion of humans were above average, both in verbal and nonverbal skills *and* in assertiveness and aggressiveness. These associations suggest both a means and a motive for children's self-representation in dreams via animal surrogates. Yet these associations can only go so far in making the children's reports of dream animals look credible.

We also made another finding that points in an opposite direction, namely, that the most prolific animal reporters were the two young children mentioned above as possible dream confabulators, since their preschool REM recall was relatively high and later dropped off, while other children generally showed slow but steady improvement in reporting REM dreams over the course of the longitudinal study. I know that there is much discussion in psychological theory and data from outside dream psychology about why young children might or should be expected to dream often of animals. I also am aware that home-collected or school-collected dream samples contain much animal dreaming, especially among preschoolers (Van de Castle, 1971). But even though the longitudinal findings support these expectations and replicate these data, I must confess that I remain somewhat uneasy about whether preschoolers' animal reports generally reflect actual animal dreams. In collecting such reports in the laboratory I experienced a mild disbelief that I've never quite been able to shake.

The body-state sleep or fatigue dreams would seem even more suspect. Obviously the children, in their reports, confused what they really were doing before being waked up—sleeping—with what they were imagining they were doing, if in fact they were imagining or dreaming anything at all. So maybe the young boy was dreaming that he was in a barber shop, but whatever he was doing there, it wasn't sleeping—that's something he realized he really was doing only after he woke up.

Once again, however, both psychological theory and additional observations are there to suggest that the suspicious preschooler dream phenomenon may in fact be real. The theory is that preschoolers are self-centered or unable to de-center from current reality (Piaget & Inhelder, 1969). Thus their imagining, if any, may be bound to their own current situation. On these grounds, it is not unreasonable to assume that children's first nocturnal efforts at performing human-kind's most masterful act of decentering from ourselves to construct a wholly imaginary reality, namely, the phenomenon we know as dreaming, would retain ties to their real situation in a way that our dreams typically don't.

Among academics in the field of child or developmental psychology, the notion of egocentrism as a defining feature in the preschool years has fallen out of fashion. Nonetheless, the field may have lost its bearing on this issue. While contemporary scholars focus on the discovery of heretofore unrecognized intellectual competencies at earlier and earlier ages, the general public is less and less able to understand the obvious fact that young children think differently and much less capably than we do. The reason the concept of egocentrism lasted so long in child psychology, and why there are pockets of resistance still defending it, is that it makes plausible sense of these differences.

The longitudinal study data, moreover, paint a rather impressive picture of preschool children who dreamed relatively often of self-ascribed body states and relatively seldom of motor or interpersonal acts by other dream characters. Such children were both older and smarter than their peers. Their smartness showed up as skills in visual-spatial imagining, represented, for instance, by the Block Design test of the Wechsler series of intelligence tests (raw scores on this test are among the most consistent predictors of dreaming skills in later childhood). Imagining yourself sleeping in a place where you aren't probably doesn't seem like a big leap forward in dream competence, but in fact it lay within the competence of only the brightest and oldest of preschoolers. The origin of real, as opposed to surrogate (animal), self-involvement in preschoolers' dreams may therefore reside in quintessentially static scenes of the dreamer's own ongoing sleep activity.

Mental Imagery

Here it may be well to reiterate a finding from adult cases of brain damage or retinal lesions: that dreaming depends not on how well one perceives the world, but on how well one can recreate or simulate that world mentally. Viewing both the negative features and the emerging positive features of preschoolers' REM dream reports, I am led to suggest that preschoolers *generally* (that is, not just in their dreaming alone) have difficulty in mentally imagining an active self or any kind of movement or ongoing interaction. This doesn't mean that they can't talk about self or action; clearly they can and do. But an inability accurately to reflect in mental imagery on such things may be part of the explanation why preschoolers think differently and less well than we do.

In the "mental rotation" test (see Shepard & Cooper, 1982) we gave to children in the cross-sectional study, the subject is asked to determine whether two figures are the same or different, and the time it takes to make that judgment is his or her score of interest. Our figures were wooden monkeys, each of which could have either its right arm or its left arm raised. In some cases, both monkeys were in the upright position. More often, however, one monkey deviated from the upright position at some specified angle. With adult observers, the typical finding is that the farther the second monkey is rotated away from the upright position of the first, the longer it takes to respond "same" or "different." The interpretation typically given to this delay is that, before comparing the two figures, the observer "mentally rotates" the angled figure to the upright position, and that such rotation takes longer the greater the initial discrepancy of the two figures. The discovery of the empirical relationship between angular discrepancy and response time, and the proposal of its hypothetical basis, are rightly viewed as one of the major recent successes in objectively studying inner mental processes.

Although slower than adults, even young children can give accurate "same" and "different" responses. Yet they do not reliably show the empirical relationship between degrees of rotation and reaction time, that is, they don't seem mentally to be rotating the figure the same way adults are assumed to be doing. And children who did seem to be rotating the figure mentally were no more accurate in "same" versus "different" responses than those who didn't (Foulkes, Sullivan, Hollifield, & Bradley, 1989; Foulkes & Hollifield, 1989). These findings suggest that young children generally don't, and don't have to, use mental imagery to solve visual-spatial problems. But adults do seem to use that medium. Why? Perhaps because they have something the typical 4- or 5-year-old doesn't have: the potential for mentally imagining movement in visual-spatial imagery. That interpretation certainly is consistent with another reliable indicator of mental imagery phenomena in early childhood: REM dream reporting.

Without recognizing it, the preschoolers were telling me about their skills in visual-spatial imagining. *They* thought that they were describing events, events they perhaps thought were as real as any others. But since these events were, in fact, entirely imagined, the children were unwittingly also describing the range and limits of their visual-spatial imagination. And, as surely as adults in mental-rotation experiments, they were revealing something about their ability to recreate or simulate reality in their own imagination. The REM dream reports of preschoolers show that that ability is different from, and much more limited than, our own. This conclusion explains why one piece of received wisdom about young children's dreams—that they are rich and imaginative—is wrong.

Feelings

Another item of received wisdom challenged by the preschoolers' REM dream reports is that children's dreams tend to be very frightening. In fact, in 67 dream reports from all sleep stages—REM and non-REM—fear was *never* reported, and in only 1 of those 67 reports did the dream self receive an "unfavorable outcome," the description our content-analysis system gave to what more commonly might be called a "bad" dream.

Children rarely reported feelings of any kind in their dreams. One problem here, of course, is that they themselves generally weren't in the dream scene, so that the kind of involvement that we associate with emotional dreaming wasn't present for them. Also, from the typical animal and body-state dream fragments that I have mentioned, you can see that what they did report dreaming wouldn't seem to call for any accompanying feeling.

But the real problem with the expectation that children's dreams will be dripping with feelings, mostly unpleasant ones at that, is that it starts with the wrong assumptions. It is assumed either that feeling-states have some primary or special role in generating dreams (stemming from psychiatry's century-long infatuation with psychoanalysis), or that feelings are a "natural" part of dreaming, a "given" in the sense that dreaming itself also often is considered to be (see Chapter 1).

The preschoolers' dreams belie these assumptions. Indeed, a moment's reflection on our own dream life should give us much reason to doubt the naturalness of feelings accompanying dream events. The major anomaly in adult REM-sleep dreaming is that we often dream, without feeling accompaniment, events that, if experienced in waking life, *would* be accompanied by feelings (Foulkes, Sullivan, Kerr, & Brown, 1988). This suggests that it is not easy even for adults to generate feelings appropriate to dream events (and our dream feelings are, contrary to another psychoanalytic stereotype, overwhelmingly appropriate to the dream context). So how "natural" can it be for very young children, who don't seem to have much overall dream competency in the first place, to call up the requisite feeling accompaniments as well?

The advent of feelings in dreams is a step in development. Supplying event-accompaniments such as either feelings or more purely cognitive reflections is something that children don't do until, after age 7 or so, they are able to represent themselves actively in dreams. Moreover, our findings show that the traits of those children who first and best fill out their dreams with feelings have little to do with their waking feeling life, but much to do with their waking cognitive competence. In other words, the ability to supply dreams with feelings is not so much driven by emotional development as it is permitted by cognitive development: it is part of becoming a better, more competent dreamer. And it is certainly no more a "given" in early development than is dreaming itself.

But what is the experiential source for the widespread expectation of a frightening dream world for young children? It surely isn't just a pure delusion. Partly, I think, it lies in our own very imperfectly (and hopelessly incompletely) remembered dreams of childhood. Many of these memories, however vivid and real they seem to the adult, are probably no more valid than Jean Piaget's (1962, p. 187n–188n) vivid recollection of a childhood kidnapping that never happened, nor than many of the "recovered" memories that now bedevil American family life. That a memory is experienced as real, that we believe with all our heart and soul that some event happened just as we remember it, we now know is absolutely no guarantee of its validity (see the posthumous work of Nicholas Spanos [1996], which vividly documents the unreliability of memory, the relative independence of confidence and accuracy in memory, and the experimental creation and everyday incidence of wholly false memories). The remembered childhood dream is the prototype of Dream B discussed in Chapter 2; in all likelihood, it has little if anything to do with childhood sleep experiences.

Our personal-historical memory is not constructed like some idealized PBS or BBC documentary that purports to tell us what "really" happened. It is more in the service of validating our current account of who we'd like to think we are, and, if facts don't fit, facts be damned. A large part of the reason Freud became lost in his theorizing is that he attempted to reconstruct the child's world from the memories of his adult patients, rather than from observations of children themselves. For the child's world of dreaming we now have the more direct data, and no need to rely on highly fallible later memories of adults.

But another source of the expectation of frightening dreams, of course, lies in our experience as parents. For most parents, children's nighttime mental life rarely intrudes. But when it does, it often seems to be in the context of anxiety, if not downright terror. As I already had occasion to note, however, many behavioral signs taken to indicate children's dream life probably have nothing whatsoever to do with it. The most spectacular of these signs is the "night terror," in which children awaken, typically early in the night, in intense fear and agitation (Kales, Jacobson, & Kales, 1969). Night terrors arise in the deepest and most dreamless sleep of the night, and any accompanying hallucinations or delusions come from faulty awakening from such sleep, not from any ongoing dream. In addition, there are sampling problems in reconstructing children's typical dream life from a few remembered-because-they-scared-me dreams.

But there's another factor, I think, in the difference between the laboratory picture of a placid dream life and the parental picture of a disturbed dream life for preschoolers. That factor has to do with how children awaken. A "crisp" laboratory awakening is externally guided; it is rapid, it is progressive; and the interviewer immediately orients the child to what happened just before awakening. A child's home awakening is internally guided (to the extent it has any real guidance); it is slow with lapses back toward sleep; and the child much more likely orients to the here-and-now than to the where-I've-just-been. The here-and-now is dark; it is quiet; and one is alone. *It* likely *is* frightening. Any remembered dream becomes part of this frightening here-and-now. In this way, dreams come to seem to be the cause of feelings that originally had nothing to do with them during sleep itself.

What Dreaming Does

Amid all my discussion of how the dreams of preschoolers seem to be different, and less accomplished, than ours, there is one important similarity of their dreaming to our own. In each case, mental life during sleep is not a direct reproduction or a direct anticipation of waking life experiences. Children's dreams, like ours, are not simple rememberings, and they are not realistic anticipations. Their dream life, like ours, puts events and actors and objects together in novel and unanticipated ways. It puts things together that, by waking standards, don't belong together, such as a fishbowl by the side of a river or a boy sleeping in a barber shop.

There's an important clue, I think, in this similarity of the dreaming process, from its earliest recordable moments to its latest, as to what dreaming is all about. What dreaming does is to take separate and sometimes disparate bits of information and knowledge and put them together in a novel, but generally coherent, comprehensible, and realistic synthesis that makes them seem as if they in fact belonged together. A fishbowl and a river are not direct mental associates, but neither are they re-mote ones. They share the property of "fish containers." They are not generally found side by side, but it involves no contra-diction of reality to imagine that they could be. In its most primitive form, the dream contrives to bring together in a plausible, if not always likely, situation images of physical things or events that ordinarily (that is, in waking life) would not be seen or thought of or imagined simultaneously. For pre-schoolers, the coherence or information-integration of dream-ing is mostly only at the level of the cohesive single image.

Later, of course, for adults and even for young school-aged children, the coherence of dreaming takes on a new aspect: imagery coheres over time, as story lines and narratives replace the static image. What happens at moment $n + 1$ in a dream is strongly constrained by what happened at moment n. But this change is an addition rather than a qualitative shift, because momentary imagery in the dream narrative still effectively in-tegrates people, places, and things that don't necessarily "be-long" together, and because the same criteria of coherence and comprehensibility and effective reality-simulation still apply, only they now operate on a temporally broader stage.

For both the young child and the adult, then, the raw mate-rial of the dream seems to be ideation that doesn't naturally fit together. The activity of dreaming is what makes these pieces seem to fit together in a coherent and plausible way. Dream-ing, which many of us think of as inherently disorganized, is, by its very nature, an organizing process, and its notion of what constitutes successful organization consists of the same standards as prevail in waking mental life. If there is a differ-ence in how well these standards typically are met, that is, if there is any residual truth in the notion that dreams are more disorganized or less coherent than waking mental experience, then that may reflect the more scattered sources with which dreaming deals, rather than any bias of the dreaming process towards chaos. Dreaming itself seems to be an extraordinarily orderly process.

5

~

Ages Five to Nine

Dreaming Develops

The major changes that take dreaming from the rudimentary form it assumes in the preschool years—dreams are brief and infrequent; they focus on body states; their imagery is static—to the mature form in adulthood take place between ages 5 and 9. These changes occur in two stages. *First*, dream reports become longer, but not more frequent, and now describe social interaction and the kind of movement that suggests kinematic rather than static imaging; still lacking, however, is active participation in dream events by the dreamer herself or himself. *Next*, dream reports become more frequent as well as longer and narratively more complex, and active self-participation becomes a general possibility, along with, for the first time, the reliable attribution to the self of feelings and thoughts occurring in the dream in response to dream events.

If we call the results of the preschoolers *Stage 1* of dream development, then let's call the two stages just mentioned *Stage 2* and *Stage 3*. These stages were present in the longitudinal study, where changes in the dreaming of individual children

Table 3. Stages of REM-dream development

	Stages			
	0	1	2	3
Approximate ages	0–3	3–5	5–7	7–9
Dream frequency	none	rare	rare, but increasing	relatively frequent
Dream form	—	isolated event	simple event sequence	complex narrative
Dream imagery	—	static	kinematic	kinematic
Active self-participation	—	absent	absent	present

could be observed, and they were largely replicated in the cross-sectional study, where different children were compared at different ages. In the longitudinal study, 13 of 14 children reliably showed the progression from Stage 1 to Stage 2, and 12 of 14 children the progression from Stage 2 to Stage 3. Given the problems of underreporting and overreporting in working with children, especially at very young ages, these numbers must be judged as very impressive, particularly in documenting a picture of dream development that neither I nor the children nor their parents at all expected. In the longitudinal study, the typical age at which a child passed into Stage 2 was 7.1, and the typical age at which a child passed into Stage 3 was 7.4, suggesting that Stage 2 is rather brief.

The cross-sectional study, during which children were studied within a month of birthdays ranging from 5 to 8 years of age, obviously was less sensitive to changes within a given birth year. Here it was observed that children first reliably reported kinematic imagery—indexing movement and inter-action content—at age 7, but did not reliably report active self-participation until age 8. The big picture that emerges from both studies, then, is that somewhere around the age of 7, children become capable of imagining small sequences of events and activities in their dreams, but it is only somewhat later that they become capable of inserting a self character into this newly activated dream world.

Longitudinal Study at Ages 5 to 7
REM Dream Recall

When studied in their third study year, the former preschoolers now generally ranged in age, at the year's beginning, from ages 5 to 6 (and at the year's end, from ages 6 to 7). Compared at this age to their earlier performance, they did not report dreams on a significantly greater percent of REM-sleep awakenings, although the typical child now did report dreams on 31% of such awakenings. When dreams were reported, however, they were significantly longer than before, substantive word counts having almost tripled since the first study year, from a median report length of 14 words to 41 words.

The children with especially frequent REM dream reports were now, more encouragingly than when studied two years earlier, those gifted at visual-spatial skills as measured by Block Design and other tests. At all subsequent age levels in the longitudinal study, up to ages 13 to 15, some cognitive variable positively correlated with rates of REM dream reporting, and Block Design was the variable most often so correlated. (In the Block Design subtest of the Wechsler Intelligence Scales, you are shown a picture of a colored pattern and asked to reconstruct it with all-red blocks, all-white blocks, and half-red, half-white blocks.)

The kinds of visual-spatial skills assessed by tests such as Block Design have little to do with abilities to remember or to describe visual patterns. More plausibly, they are skills operative in mentally imagining such patterns in the first place. In view of the correlation with this skill, and for other reasons, I believe that, from age 5 on, the rate at which children *reported* dreaming on REM awakenings in the longitudinal study accurately indexes the rate at which they *experienced or created* dreams. It was not the case, at this and succeeding ages, that the most frequent dream reporters were the children with the best memories or vocabularies or descriptive skills. Rather, it was children who were best at the kind of skills that would be involved in imagining dream worlds in the first place who reported dreams most often. These findings refute the counterargument that my data are artifactual, that children aren't becoming better dreamers, they are just becoming better able to tell the dreams they have been having all along.

Another reason for believing that tests like Block Design correlate with the actual generation of dreams, and that such generation is still relatively infrequent at ages 5 to 7, came from observing two boys added to our older longitudinal study group at ages 11 and 12. These boys, brothers, had, for their age, typical verbal and memory skills, and performed adequately at school. Their results in our test program, however, revealed that they had a specific cognitive deficit in visual-spatial skill. As young adolescents, they had Block Design scores only comparable to those of 5- to 7-year-olds in the younger longitudinal study group. They also dream-reported like the 5- to 7-year-olds, having extremely low REM dream recall. In their case, even more clearly than for the 5- to 7-year-olds, it can't be that the children are having dreams but simply can't remember or describe them very well. It seems much more likely that they were simply not having dreams, or not having very memorable dreams. This, in turn, suggests that the same must be true of the 5- to 7-year-olds, with their comparably low, but typical for their age, Block Design scores.

Thus, although we obviously can't be completely sure that young children's failure to report dreams means that they're just not having them, rather than merely underreporting them, the Block Design evidence strongly suggests that that is the case. Children do not dream, or do not dream very well, until they have achieved a certain level of competence in visual-spatial mental manipulation, and this competence is reflected in raw scores on such tests as Block Design.

Non-REM Dream Recall

I have mentioned that most, but not all, awakenings in the longitudinal study were scheduled for REM sleep. One reason for scheduling non-REM awakenings is for "control" purposes. Since adults generally recall dreams more often from the more cortically activated REM sleep than from non-REM sleep, you want to see if children will show the same pattern. If not, you have reason to be suspicious of the reports you are collecting. As I've indicated, even the preschoolers passed this test of dream-report credibility.

However, there's another reason, generally less well known, for awakening children from non-REM sleep. Although popularizations of dream research often tend to gloss over this fact, significant dreaming in adults occurs outside REM sleep (see, for example, Foulkes, 1985, ch. 2), and, except for its briefer nature, such dreaming seems qualitatively indistinguishable from REM dreaming (Antrobus, 1983; Foulkes & Schmidt, 1983). The very same system or systems that are responsible for REM dreaming also are active in much of our non-REM sleep, just not so intensely. Consequently, tracing the development of non-REM dreaming in childhood becomes as relevant as finding the origins of REM dreaming.

Between ages 5 and 7 in the longitudinal study, non-REM dreaming sends its first reliable blip across the developmental screen. While reliable, it is not much: the typical child reports dreams on only 6% of non-REM awakenings (and as both before and later, the non-REM report rate is significantly less than that for REM sleep). Two interesting observations were made about 5- to 7-year-old children who were relatively high in non-REM dream reporting: they were also high-rate REM dream reporters, and they were gifted in the visual-spatial skills that characterized these high-REM reporters. As with adults, even in these young children REM and non-REM dreaming were not qualitatively different. Rather, they went hand-in-hand, and if you believe either one takes place at ages 5 to 7 (and we have seen that there is good evidence in each case), you have to believe in both.

In pondering why credibility first can be accorded to most dream reports after age 5, one naturally thinks of school. It is a chicken-and-egg problem, perhaps. Do we initiate formal schooling because children now are ready to become objective, or does their thinking veer toward objectivity because of school? There is some evidence for the efficacy of schooling, but the more remarkable observation is that, in societies across the world, the 5 to 7 period is viewed as one in which children are ready to assume social roles and responsibility (see Sameroff & Haith, 1996). In our society, this readiness coincides with the start of formal training in objectively reporting personally uninteresting information to relative strangers (in other words, schooling). This experience must have considerable positive effect on children's performance in dream reporting on laboratory awakenings.

REM Dream Content

More detailed review of content-analysis category changes in children's dreams between ages 3–5 and 5–7 showed significant decreases in sleep/fatigue themes (which no longer were the province of the intellectually precocious), and increases in social-interaction activities and settings. Interestingly, animals persisted as dream characters (although they no longer held center stage), and frequent animal dreamers tended to be the same children who had such dreams in the first study year; again, they were relatively skilled cognitively. These data argue against my own expressed reservations, and for the reality of relatively frequent animal dreaming from ages 3 to 7.

The significant increases in social interaction within the dream content were, as the big picture sketched out above would suggest, generally limited to social interaction by characters other than the dreamer. While both prosocial and hostile acts by *others* showed such increases, neither category increased significantly for the dreamer's *self* character, mainly because there was still little dreamer participation in dream events.

In general, the specific content of children's dreams is less interesting from a viewpoint on dreaming-as-process, than it is from a viewpoint on the dream-as-product. But one question about children's dreams from ages 5 or 6 on is relevant to understanding the process of dreaming. On what basis is information selected for dream portrayal? Is waking experience selected for dream representation on the basis of its frequency of occurrence, for instance, or on the basis of its interest or meaning for the child? Two test cases are schoolwork and television, both the watching and the watched. These consume, from age 5 or 6 on, much of children's time, the one because adults insist, and the other because often there isn't anyone else to play with or anything better to do. Neither ever figures at all prominently in children's dreams.

Features that assume priority in children's dreams are recreational activities, events, and settings. It has been said that play is the work of childhood; the earnestness with which it is sought, almost always in a peer context, does suggest its centrality to growing up. It is also central in children's dreams. The more general point is that, for children as for adults, dream stories do not depend on what the dreamers have done or how long they have spent doing it. What is dreamed reflects not daytime behavior, but one's interpretation and evaluation of that behavior and of waking life more generally. Dreaming starts from the mind and its organization, not from the world and its organization.

As at ages 3 to 5, there was no evidence at ages 5 to 7 for the popular stereotype, based on highly selective and distorted spontaneous dream samples taken at home, that children's dreams are generally frightening. Most of the new interaction content involved positive relations with people or objects.

Only 1 dream out of every 4 included aggression, and the dreamer character rarely was either the initiator or the recipient of such aggression. Given the relative absence of the dreamer, there was little feeling or cognition in children's dream reports, and the feelings described were generally not unpleasant. Of 87 dreams reported from all sleep stages, there were only 2 in which the dreamer described being afraid during the dream.

At ages 5 to 7, children reported more unfamiliar male characters than they had at ages 3 to 5. This is of some interest in the present context, because it is often thought that young children find unfamiliar characters frightening (a bogeyman, for example). And the same line of thinking that finds it "natural" that young children should dream often and richly, also expects that they naturally will be able to conceive and portray figures of whom they will be frightened.

But the data of the longitudinal study suggest that it is not at all natural for young dreamers to create unfamiliar characters or settings in their dreams. At ages 5 to 7, when dream-report credibility first seems well established, and at subsequent ages, dream "distortions" of this sort seemed to be a general property of children's dreaming. That is, if a child dreamed relatively often of unfamiliar characters, he or she also dreamed relatively often of unfamiliar settings. What is especially interesting at ages 5 to 7 is that it was cognitively gifted children who did so most often. Dream distortion, the ability to imagine the unfamiliar, is not a "given" in early childhood; it takes time and an accompanying increase in cognitive skill for it to develop.

Clinical dream theories such as Freud's (1900; see also Foulkes, 1978, ch. 4, and a set of contemporary reviews edited by Kramer, 1994) suggest that we distort in dreams because we have to, because we are trying to repress something we really don't want to know. The longitudinal study's data, on the other hand, suggest that we first distort in dreams when we are cognitively able to do so; that distortion is a developing skill whereby we can mix together different mental contents with resulting well-formed, novel dream imagery.

One nice example of the difference between looking at dream competencies as a "given" and distortion as motivated self-deception, on the one hand, and seeing dream competencies, including the portrayal of novelty, as slowly developing skills, on the other, uses Freud's account of a dream supposedly experienced by his patient, the "Wolf Man," at age 4 (see Gardiner, 1971). The Wolf Man reported this dream to Freud many years after its purported occurrence. The child was in bed (body-state of sleep, passive self); a window opened to reveal white wolves (animal characters), sitting in a big walnut tree (static imagery).

Freud, who evidently thought that the four-year-old's dream skills are almost as good as ours, saw the distinctive features of this dream as motivated attempts to disguise other underlying contents. The immobility of the wolves, for instance, was interpreted as the reversal of some scene of frantic activity seen by the child in his waking life. Freud concluded that the 4-year-old Wolf Man must have seen his parents in the act of sexual intercourse. When the dream is interpreted through the developing-ability hypothesis, however, the child is seeing immobility because he literally cannot yet imagine activity, not because he's trying to deny it. When one starts by believing that anything is possible in children's dreaming, one can readily believe in both dream monsters and bogeyman and in repressed complexes. When one starts with the much more empirically defensible belief that children's dream competency is limited by their general cognitive competency, then these phenomena are as little believable as they are scarcely observable in reality.

Longitudinal Study at Ages 7 to 9

In their final study year, the younger longitudinal study group generally comprised 7- and 8-year-olds at the year's beginning and 8- and 9-year-olds at the year's end. As mentioned, 7 additional girls were studied in this year only, yielding an overall sample of 14 girls, 7 from the original group, and 7 boys, all from the original group recruited as preschoolers. Longitudinal changes, of course, could only be evaluated with the original group.

Dream Recall

These changes included a continuing increase in the rate of dream reporting on REM-sleep awakenings, the typical child now reporting dreams on 43% (versus the earlier 31%) of these awakenings. Interestingly, the stronger trend was for an increase in non-REM recall, from a typical 6% to 22%. This increase resulted mainly from non-REM sleep awakenings toward morning, when non-REM sleep is particularly light. Increases in REM recall also came largely from awakenings later in the night. Both the non-REM and the REM results parallel observations made with adults, and support the credibility of the children's dream reporting. Although correlated with REM recall, non-REM recall occurred significantly less often than did REM recall, and, as throughout the project for both study groups, produced significantly shorter reports as well. These results, of course, also parallel adult observations, and therefore add further credibility to the children's reports.

While increasing, the 7- to 9-year-olds' dream reporting on REM awakenings still did not approach typical adult levels (85–90%). In fact, a comparison of the 7- to 9-year-olds in their final study year with the 9- to 11-year-olds in their first study year (79% recall for the typical child) showed a significant difference. With REM recall, and, on my account, REM dreaming itself, still a relatively difficult achievement at ages 7 to 9, the best-achieving children were the ones better skilled at tests of visual-spatial mental manipulation, such as Block Design, and also at verbally mediated tests of general knowledge. Waking measures of memory skill seemed to be quite unrelated to rate of dream reporting.

Another clear finding during the general increase in REM and non-REM recall from ages 5 to 9 was that it seemed to have nothing to do with children's waking adjustment or anxieties. It isn't personal problems or conflicts that *impel* children to produce more complicated dreams. Rather, it's the well-known spurt in cognitive competence ("the 5 to 7 shift": White, 1965; Sameroff & Haith, 1996) that seems to *permit* children to become more accomplished dreamers.

Dreaming: How Long Versus How Often?

And how, precisely, did the longitudinally-studied children become better dreamers between ages 5 to 7 and ages 7 to 9?

First, they reported longer dreams, the typical child having REM reports of 72 words in length. With this increase in length, I also observed increasing narrative complexity, but, in the longitudinal study, there was no way to quantify or verify that impression. That step was taken in the subsequent cross-sectional study.

The length of REM dream reports did not correlate, at any age level in either longitudinal study group, with visual-spatial measures such as Block Design. The growth in dream report length in early childhood does not, then, seem to reflect the same kind of mental development that underlies the growth in the frequency with which dreams are reported, and, again on my account, experienced. It may be that length of report depends more on continuously growing competencies in attention, memory, and descriptive skill, while frequency of reporting is more closely related to visual-spatial skills that make dreaming itself possible. This is consistent with the different growth patterns for dream recall and dream length.

Some evidence for this disjunction also was observed earlier in the longitudinal study, at ages 5 to 7. At those ages, while *frequency* of REM dream reporting was related, as we have seen, to visual-spatial skills, children with the *longest* REM dream reports were identified in the daytime test program as having good descriptive skills and language quality. And the cross-sectional study data also suggested different cognitive correlates for dream frequency and dream length.

Active Self Representation

As the "big picture" outlined at the start of this chapter pointed out, the content analysis in the longitudinal study indicated a significant increase at ages 7 to 9 in *self*-representation, the self performing a variety of dream activities. With the increase in self-representation came a corresponding decrease in animal characters, and those children who still did dream relatively frequently of animals were younger and less gifted cognitively than their peers. These findings do seem to suggest that animal characters stand in for the dreamer before the dreamer can be directly and actively represented in dreams. It is noteworthy also that the significant increase in self-participation in dreams from ages 7 to 9 was in prosocial behavior rather than in hostile or unpleasant situations. When a self character does finally appear on the dream scene, it is in the same kind of well-controlled scenarios previously extended to other dream characters.

With the self character came some of its characteristic states, such as thoughts and feelings. Thoughts within the dream were noted in roughly 10% of REM reports. Although the thoughts of the dreamer character generally were verbal, children with dreamer thoughts were especially skilled in visual-spatial reasoning. So too were children who felt happy in their dreams: being happy in waking life doesn't predict that you'll be happy in your dreams while growing up, but being skilled in the visual-spatial area does.

Happy feelings were the most frequent feelings at ages 7 to 9, and were reported in about 15% of children's REM dream reports. Fear and anger make their first real appearance in the dreams of the younger longitudinal group at ages 7 to 9, with fear being more prevalent, appearing in about 10% of children's dreams. This 10% figure also characterized the older longitudinal group from ages 9 to 15. Thus there wasn't much of a "psychological" dimension in the 7- to 9-year-olds' dreams.

For them, as is also generally true for us, dreams are more action than reflection or feeling. But when the psychological dimension first reliably enters children's dream experiences, it seems to do so most often for children whose visual-spatial skills permit it.

Cross-Sectional Study at Ages 5 to 8
Dreaming: How Long Versus How Often?

We did not have an index of narrative complexity for dreams from the longitudinal study. Word counts, as you may imagine, are a very imperfect reflection of skill in making up stories. Consequently, in the cross-sectional study, we had judges evaluate the narrative quality of dream reports, and of stories children told when they were awake as well. The obvious goal was to describe narrative development in children's dreams between ages 5 and 8, and to see how well that reflected children's waking narrative skills.

We found that the big jump in dream narration occurred between age 7 and age 8. By one measure, this shift was from a single story unit—a scene or situation—to several such units that were continuous with one another. By another measure, the shift was from a simple sequence of otherwise unrelated actions to a sequence of action and reaction to prior actions, with the possibility of one action being performed with the *intent* of producing some effect.

The narrative quality of REM reports was the *only* dream variable to show a significant and steady effect of age of the child in the cross-sectional study, and it was found to be related most strongly to the waking cognitive variable most strongly related to age: language skill. (This parallels the longitudinal observation at ages 5 to 7.) Dream narration did *not* have visual-spatial correlates.

The frequency of reporting dreams on REM awakenings, by contrast, *was* strongly related to visual-spatial skills: Block Design was its strongest cognitive correlate, and mental-rotation scores also were significantly related to rate of dreaming. Language skills as measured by IQ-type tests were not related to frequency of dream reporting, but waking measures of narrative complexity were. Interestingly, dream-narrative complexity was *not* related to the complexity of waking narratives. The report-rate versus narration separation observed in the cross-sectional group thus brings additional evidence that simply having a dream depends on different skills than does having a formally accomplished dream.

Visual-spatial skills such as those employed in Block Design clearly are related to making and being able to report dreams, while simple verbal skills are not. The cross-sectional study adds the observation that a high-level operation on verbal contents, namely waking-narrative skill, is related to making and remembering dreams. That is not surprising, because storytelling and dreaming are two of the greatest forms of human narration. It *would* be surprising if they were *not* related. Whether the narrative quality of the dream depends on the dreamer's waking verbal intelligence is more problematic: since dream-narrative quality was the only variable to increase significantly over the span from ages 5 to 8, and since verbal IQ showed the strongest age-related increase among cognitive variables, the relation of the two variables to each other may not have direct causal significance. They may just be two phenomena, one in nocturnal cognition and the other in day-time cognition, that happen to improve steadily with age and thus seem more intimately interrelated than they really are.

Frequency of reporting and of experiencing dreams does not steadily improve with age, however. In fact, in the cross-sectional study it did not improve at all from ages 5 to 8. The typical REM recall rate from ages 5 to 8 was only 20%, 2 dreams from the 10 awakenings made for each child. I believe that, had we also studied 9-year olds, an age-related increase would have been observed. But even in the longitudinal study, the increase in REM dream reporting from ages 5–7 to 7–9 reached only what is very generously called statistically marginal significance. Clearly, children's dream recall does increase between ages 3 to 9, but the interesting observation is that this increase does not mirror steady increases in general waking cognitive competence nearly so well as do word-count or narrative-quality measures of the dreams that are reported. From all my data, the suggestion is that dreaming best reflects the development of a specific cognitive competence, indexed by certain kinds of tests of visual-spatial imagination, leading to the conclusion that such imagination must be a critical skill in dream-making.

Why were recall rates so low in the cross-sectional study? There's no way of knowing for sure, but one factor may be a change in interview strategy from the longitudinal study. Bearing in mind that the major problem with young children in the earlier study seemed to have been overreporting—telling a "dream" when one wasn't there—I stressed the acceptability and correctness of a "no dream" response if none could be recalled. I told the children that each awakening was like an experiment, that neither I nor they could tell in advance if they were dreaming, so we would just have to wait and see what happened each time they were awakened.

Image Quality

The quality of the dream image (static versus kinematic) did not have significant cognitive correlates over the whole span of ages (5–8) in the cross-sectional study, but Block Design did show "marginal" significance in predicting such quality. But at age 8, when self-representation first became reliable and general, visual-spatial skills (though not, in these cases, the specific Block Design measure) did predict both kinematic imaging and active self-representation. This corroborates the longitudinal findings: when children first achieve some new dreaming skill, those who do so first or best are the ones skilled in visual-spatial imaging.

The mental-rotation test, which we included because it seemed specifically to assess waking skill in kinematic imagery, proved of no use in predicting the image quality of dreams. Although we couldn't demonstrate a direct connection between waking and dreaming image quality, we did find, in support of suggestions by the Genevan psychologists Jean Piaget and Barbel Inhelder (1971), that waking kinematic imaging is not already well developed at age 5 but develops, rather, between ages 5 and 8 (Foulkes, Sullivan, Hollifield, & Bradley, 1989). This is also, of course, what REM dream reports tell us about sleeping kinematic imaging. In comparison, received wisdom in American developmental psychology (see Mandler, 1983) has been that kinematic imaging is a much earlier achievement than Piaget and Inhelder thought and than my data show.

Credibility

One of the shortcuts necessitated by the low funding for the cross-sectional study was the elimination of non-REM awakenings. Without them, however, how could report credibility be gauged? As it turned out, one unanticipated opportunity for testing the children's recall did emerge from another aspect of our low budget; it came from my working alone as sleep-watcher and interviewer.

In the longitudinal study, REM awakenings had been made at set time intervals into REM periods, *if* eye movements were occurring. (Rapid eye movements are intermittent, rather than continuous, during REM sleep.) If eye movements weren't occurring at that moment, I waited until the next eye movement. Thus all REM awakenings in the longitudinal study were "phasic" awakenings, made at phasic eye-movement bursts during the "tonic" background conditions of REM sleep. Since most awakenings were made via intercoms, they were more or less concurrent with REM bursting. Even the bedside interviews at younger ages could be made quickly, because the bedrooms were easy to reach from the control center where I watched the polygraph recordings of REM sleep.

In the cross-sectional study, however, the bedrooms were farther away and not so easily reached, and as I stood outside the door to the child's room, I had no helpers to signal me that a REM burst had just happened. Awakenings in the cross-sectional study were therefore scheduled after so many minutes of REM sleep, whatever was happening physiologically at that particular clock time.

The reason phasic awakenings were specified in the longitudinal study was because it seems likely that, especially for young children whose dreaming might not be very well developed, dreaming might be most intense and therefore most memorable during eye-movement bursts. In the cross-sectional study I was able to put this idea to test (Foulkes & Bradley, 1989). Fifteen or twenty seconds or so away from the polygraph, out in a long hallway leading to the children's bedroom, I had no idea, as the specified moment of awakening came, whether the child was then showing eye movements or not. As it turned out, on 567 awakenings eye movements did occur in the 15 seconds prior to my opening the door to the child's bedroom and calling her or his name, and on 210 awakenings there were no eye movements in that 15 second interval. Recall, pooled over all subjects, was 26.5% on eye-movement awakenings and 18.6% on awakenings with no eye movement. This difference was statistically significant, and it does suggest report credibility, even in the absence of non-REM "controls." It also suggests a methodological factor in the lower overall REM recall of the cross-sectional study.

Active Self-Representation

Probably the most surprising and intriguing of the many unexpected findings of the longitudinal study was that it took so long for children's dreaming capacity for active, on-the-scene self-representation to develop. Given the neuropsychological evidence that imagery phenomena in dreaming are continuous with imagery phenomena in waking experience, this finding suggested the startling possibility that children can't visually imagine themselves acting in the world until ages 7 or 8. If true, that certainly would be a novel observation with seemingly immense implications for understanding the different mental worlds of early childhood and later adult life.

A first goal of the cross-sectional study, then, was to find out if the longitudinal data on self-representation were in fact correct. As I've noted, we did replicate the observation that kinematic imaging does reliably precede the ability to represent the self actively in such imagery, and confirmed that active dream self-representation develops between ages 7 and 8.

In anticipation of replicating the late appearance of active dream self-representation, the cross-sectional study test program included several waking tests of self-knowledge and self-development. As you can imagine, such tests are not easy to develop or justify. They mostly consist of standard interviews about either the "me" or the "I" identified a century ago by William James (1890). The *me* is the self as known, the self as a concept. "I'm short and a tomboy" might lie at the heart of a young girl's self-concept. The *I* is the self as knower, the agent who has a unique identity that coheres over time, who is the same boy whose mother took him to the circus two years ago.

Try operationalizing these two selves in the form of reliable and valid psychological tests, and you'll understand why only modest success has been achieved in understanding self-development (Damon & Hart, 1988). Not surprisingly, we found that results on three such tests, even when in the same supposed domain of self, were not related to one another and did not predict self-representation in REM dreaming (Foulkes, Hollifield, Bradley, Terry, & Sullivan, 1991).

I believe that an index of REM dream self-representation is inherently superior to any waking measure of self phenomena currently available, or likely to be developed soon. In describing their dreams, children are describing events in the way they believed them to happen. That's their perspective. From our perspective, they are telling us about operations they can and cannot perform in their mind's eye. And best of all, they are telling us this without even realizing it. When we have replicated and reliable evidence, from this best of all avenues to children's mental experience, suggesting a startlingly different picture of the early development of human mental life, that evidence deserves our serious attention. The evidence I refer to, of course, indicates the surprising lateness in children's development of the ability to imagine themselves as actors in their own mental imagery.

Our excursion into waking testing of self-development was not entirely fruitless. One methodological problem in trying to correlate the waking tests with REM dream self-representation across the whole age range (5–8) of the cross-sectional sample is that there aren't many claims of self-representation until age 8, while claims that *are* made at earlier ages may be invalid ones. That may well explain why visual-spatial measures correlated with active dream self-representation only at age 8.

Our test of the "I" aspect of the self (Guardo & Bohan, 1971) asked children a number of questions concerning their identity, such as: could you be another person? are you the same person now as when you were a baby? would you be the same person if you had a different name? Higher scores were given to answers judged to show a more mature understanding of the self. The most reliable jump in self-understanding on this test also occurred between ages 7 and 8. It is especially interesting to note that, while before age 8 self-understanding had correlates dominantly in language and reasoning tests, at age 8 its correlates were Block Design and accuracy in mental rotation.

Mature or relatively sophisticated characteristics of *me* knowledge on the two other self tests also had dynamic visual-spatial correlates. Thus, not only REM dream self-representation but also relatively complex and late-appearing signs of waking self-growth seem to be mediated by the same visual-spatial skills that underlie the very act of dreaming. These relationships of nocturnal and daytime self variables with visual-spatial skills are observed despite the verbal format in which test data are collected and dreams are described.

While the data of the cross-sectional self tests need to be replicated, they suggest that waking self-knowledge and dreaming self-representation may find a common basis at about age 8 in the newfound ability to simulate a self-involved world in the mind's eye. The common visual-spatial correlates of the incidence of dreaming itself, of dream self-representation, and of waking self-knowledge at age 8 surely suggest that the medium of conscious representation may be involved in the waking development as well as in the dreaming one. Another suggestive observation at age 8 was that the very best single predictor of REM recall was *not* a cognitive variable in the traditional sense, but the "I" self inquiry. The act of dreaming, of being able to act in the dream, of having a relatively mature self-identity—these phenomena seem to be interrelated, although we don't as yet know to what extent or how. But I do believe that our next great leap in understanding how we develop a conscious sense of our selfhood, that is to say, how we become fully human, will come from a setting developmental psychologists have never even considered: the sleep laboratory.

6

~

Ages Nine to Fifteen

Given the dramatic (literally!) changes in children's dreaming from ages 5 to 9, and the relatively mature form of children's dreaming by age 9, the subsequent years for which the older longitudinal group was studied could not totally match the kinds of changes in dreaming observed in the younger group. Nonetheless, the older group's data still have an interesting story to tell about the development of dreaming.

The group originally consisted of 16 children (8 girls, 8 boys) studied at approximate ages 9 to 11. In the third year of the project, generally ages 11 to 13, 14 of these children remained (8 girls, 6 boys), and 6 boys were newly recruited, giving a total sample of 20 children. In the fifth year, generally ages 13 to 15, 18 of these children remained (7 girls, 11 boys), giving us our largest year-to-year carryover for either longitudinal study group.

Dream Recall

The major jump for dreams during REM sleep seems to lie before ages 9 to 11 (specifically, between ages 7–9 and 9–11). By ages 9 to 11, the typical child in the longitudinal study was reporting dreams on REM-sleep awakenings (79%) almost as often as the typical adult (85–90%). This employs the *median* measure of averaging.

Also arguing for a relatively high-level stabilization of dreaming by ages 9 to 11 was the finding that, both for REM report frequency and for REM word counts, children in this group who scored relatively high in either variable compared to their peers in any one normative-data year also were likely to be relatively high in that same variable in the other normative-data years. Furthermore, children with frequent dream reports in each normative-data year also tended to be children with long dream reports. That is, high (or low) REM recall and REM word counts seemed to have become stable *and* interrelated personal traits by ages 9 to 11. Neither had been the case in the younger longitudinal group, in a period when both REM recall and REM word counts, and the dream phenomena they presumably represent, were undergoing unstable but dynamic increase.

In my data, the more typical measure of "average," namely, *mean*, REM recall did not budge from 66–67% from ages 9 to 15, and is somewhat lower than the value typically found for adults. I take the remaining small discrepancy with adult rates in the median measure and the somewhat larger discrepancy in the mean measure as mainly reflecting the presence of characterological dissidents in the older group. The resistance of these few to the project seemed to be part of a larger, evolving, peer-supported disdain of adult causes. While such children are not yet old and bold enough to opt out of the system, be it school or service in a research project entered with parental support, they *are* old and bold enough for resistance to solidify as persistent negativism. Ask any school teacher. In research with adults, where volunteers more likely are truly that, such negativism automatically gets selected out.

In offering this interpretation of the remaining child-adult gap in REM dream reporting, I do not entirely rule out cognitive factors that may genuinely make it difficult or impossible for some children to experience dreams. The two boys mentioned in the previous chapter, who as adolescents had specific visual-spatial deficits in skills otherwise identified with dream-making and who scarcely ever reported REM dreams, are a case in point. In studies of children you are always dealing with a more unselected or general sample than you are with adults, particularly with the much-studied college student. Almost all children go to 5th or 6th grade; relatively few go on to attend universities with sleep laboratories. Thus there will always be a greater likelihood of dream-making deficits, as well as of negativism, in child samples.

REM recall for the typical child also was 79% at ages 11 to 13, and it was 73% at ages 13 to 15. At each of these ages the brothers with the extremely low Block Design were included in the study statistics. None of the differences between age levels in the older study group for REM recall was statistically significant. Apart from the influence of the negativists and the low score of the boys with visual-spatial deficits, children's REM dream reporting was already, by ages 9 to 11, much like that of adults.

The same cannot be said of children's rate of reporting content on non-REM sleep awakenings, in conditions of lower cortical activation presumably less conducive to the generation of dreams. Typical (median) report rates for non-REM recall fluctuated nonsignificantly across study years (33% at ages 9–11, 24% at ages 11–13, and 39% at ages 13–15). While there is less agreement about typical adult values of non-REM reporting, in my substantial experience 50–60% of non-REM awakenings produce a report of some kind of preawakening mental experience. The kind of mental experience is highly variable: sometimes it is verbal and "thoughtlike"; most often it is a small-scale narrative, a scene or two of a reasonably realistic and plausible dream; occasionally it is more image than dream, with a focus on some object or person outside of any apparent narrative context (for a discussion of these possibilities, see Foulkes, 1985, ch. 2).

What is interesting about younger children's first substantial body of non-REM reports (at ages 7–11) is that they are almost exclusively of the small-scale narrative variety. Hence children's as well as adults' dreaming (rather than "thinking" or experiencing isolated and vague images) seems to be the most general and basic form of non-REM mentation.

It is worth noting that, hidden in the older children's small and nonsignificant expansion of non-REM dreaming, particularly at ages 13 to 15, is the first reporting of ideation similar to that sometimes observed in adults. Emily, one of our most intelligent and conscientious children, reported these non-REM experiences from ages 11 to 15: a shell with a lining (11–13); a piece of toast with a whole strawberry on it (11–13); a package of green paper napkins (13–15); a piece of pineapple with skin that looked like tree bark (13–15); cotton with gold braid on it (13–15). That the brightest and most scrupulous of our children started having such non-REM reports in early adolescence suggests that the ability to abstract thoughts or imagery out of a narrative format may be a late achievement in the developmental elaboration of non-REM ideation (whose earliest and most basic format is dreamlike narration on the model of REM dreaming). The presence and nature of this non-REM shift in late preadolescence and early adolescence is supported both by parallel REM-dream observations and by data and theory on waking cognitive development at this time.

Over both longitudinal study groups, the growth of non-REM dream reporting from its first appearance was consistent, rather than random. As recall increased, it required less propitious conditions. In general, of course, both REM and non-REM dreaming generally were more frequent later in the night, when there is a characteristic lightening of sleep depth. But recall from deeper non-REM sleep at ages 9–11 came to match that from lighter non-REM sleep at ages 7–9 (approximately 30%; deeper non-REM sleep is characterized by slow-frequency delta waves in the EEG pattern and occurs midway between REM periods; lighter non-REM sleep shows a relative absence of delta waves and occurs before or after REM periods). Likewise, the largest increase in non-REM recall, at ages 13–15, was attributable to increases in dream reporting from awakenings early in the night, and from deeper non-REM sleep, conditions that largely overlap in normal sleep patterning.

Consistent with the idea that the genuine generation of non-REM dreaming does increase later in childhood, non-REM dream reporting at ages 9 to 11 did *not* significantly predict such reporting at ages 13 to 15. Such year-to-year unpredictability of report rates was, as mentioned earlier, characteristic of the years—ages 3 to 9—when *REM* dreaming seemed to be increasing in frequency.

As throughout the study of both longitudinal age groups, the expected psychophysiological discriminations were demonstrated by the older children: recall was significantly higher on REM than on non-REM awakenings and was always higher, although not significantly, on light than on deep non-REM awakenings. The 9 to 15-year-olds, as the 3- to 9-year-olds, passed all standard psychophysiological tests of report credibility: they gave reports more often when such frequency was expected, in accordance with presumably valid adult reporting. The credibility of non-REM reports also is suggested, of course, by the previously noted strong positive intercorrelation of REM and non-REM reporting, which was generally observed past ages 5–7. The positive correlates of non-REM reporting also suggested the credibility of such reports. In the older group, the correlates included: cognitive skill and maturity at ages 9 to 11 (and a negative relation with a measure of waking dissimulation); social and intellectual competence at ages 11 to 13; and, at ages 13 to 15, good waking descriptive skills and memory skills and, on a psychometric test, conscientiousness.

In *REM* dream recall at ages 9 to 15, as might be expected from the stabilization of dream reporting at near-adult levels, cognition seems to make relatively less difference than other personal/social variables. Among adults, most of whom presumably *can* dream well, dream recall depends on noncognitive factors such as interest, social class, introspectiveness, and so forth. Being bright has something to do with these characteristics, of course, but it no longer seems to be a major factor;

and specifically visual-spatial skills may no longer be critical. Most everyone *can* dream; the question of who remembers them starts to reflect personality or character more than cognition.

Having said this, I must note that Block Design did significantly correlate with REM-sleep dream reporting at ages 11–13 and 13–15. But I also reiterate that this relationship was, although positive, not significant when the two brothers who had, in effect, brain lesions in certain (yet to be specified) visual-spatial areas of the brain, were excluded. If Block Design is not a general factor promoting dream recall past ages 9 to 11 or so, because it no longer measures skills at low levels that either permit or prohibit dream experience, it may remain a factor in special circumstances.

In a dissertation suggested by my data on early childhood, Stephen Butler attempted to find such circumstances among adults (Butler & Watson, 1985). He sought out, by advertising, persons who claimed that they seldom, if ever dreamed. The conventional interpretation of such claims is that these people do dream, they just don't (because of lack of interest or attention) remember their dreams. But, armed with my child data, Butler wondered if they really do dream just like the rest of us. Butler's subjects first had to demonstrate, before they were studied in a sleep laboratory, that their everyday recall as recorded in a dream-diary really was very poor. (Many people who think that they rarely, if ever, dream, soon find that they do so after all if a therapist or "group" leader turns their attention to their dream life.) When he brought validated nondreamers into a sleep laboratory, Butler was able to show that adults with low Block Design scores had significantly lower

REM report rates than did nondreamers with high Block Design scores. These two groups had been matched for verbal abilities, and did not differ significantly on neuropsychological scales of memory performance.

Thus, both for some adolescents and for some adults, Block Design and related visual-spatial skills may actually assess the capacity to make dreams. But the more general case is that, after age 9 or so, we can all experience dreams, and our recall of them no longer is diagnostic of skills of dream-making so much as of skills of dream-attending and dream-remembering. But it still is interesting to observe that, even if the conclusion depends in the oldest group on special circumstances, in all three of our child samples (younger longitudinal, young cross-sectional, older longitudinal) we did find independent evidence of the importance of certain visual-spatial skills, well assessed by Wechsler Block Design, in having and reporting dreams. (The number of supporting studies actually is four, if Butler's adult group is included.)

Active Self-Representation

From ages 7 to 9 until ages 11 to 13, there was a steady trend toward increased participation by the self in REM-dream events. At ages 11 to 13, self-participation reached parity with participation by others. In agreement with the hypothesis that animal characters may fill in for an absent self in early childhood, they decreased significantly in frequency from ages 7 to 9 to ages 9 to 11.

One finding, replicated across the two longitudinal study groups, was that, as children began to have significant levels of self-participation (ages 7 to 11), the relative absence of such participation predicted the reported unpleasantness of REM dreams. This relationship was *not* observed at ages 5 to 7 in the younger group, where self-participation was generally lacking, or at ages 11 to 13 in the older group, where self-participation achieved parity with participation by others in dream events.

Here we may have one clue to what it means to be able to insert yourself actively in your dream: you are better able to manage or control dream events to your satisfaction. If, conversely, you are not able to insert yourself actively in your dream, events are more out of your control. This evidence, from within dream life itself, suggests a more general function for self-participation in imagery and imagination: you can not only represent or simulate reality in your own mind, but also operate on such representations to produce desired outcomes. The idea that early failure to achieve active self-representation might have effects that outlive the time of such failure is suggested by the finding that experiencing unpleasantness in dreams—uniquely in our observation of global REM dream variables—became a stable personal trait from ages 9 to 11 to ages 13 to 15. That is, the frequency of unpleasant dreams at ages 9 to 11 predicted the frequency of such dreams five years later.

For the older study group as a whole, the zenith of active self-participation at ages 11 to 13 was in a context of extremely well managed dream scenarios. Neither before nor after were the children's dreams as pleasant as here. Prosocial acts in children's dreams outnumbered antisocial ones in a 2:1 ratio, and the dreamer also received more prosocial than antisocial acts from others. For dreamer initiations of activity, the prosocial to antisocial ratio was 4:1. Waking data from other research (see

Kagan & Moss, 1962) have suggested that late preadolescence sees the first grand crystallization of self, mind, character, and personality—an attainment of integrated cognitive and personality structures subject to later reorganization by adult forms of sexual and cognitive maturation, beginning in adolescence proper. My dream data certainly are consistent with this idea of a preadolescent stabilization of self-control and world mastery. And, at ages 11 to 13, the older group's REM-dream reports were as long as they ever would be, and as long as adult reports collected under comparable conditions. In late preadolescence dreaming flourishes, freed at least momentarily from constraints put upon it by cognitive immaturity.

And, because of this maturation, dream content now can begin to reflect, as it does in the adult, the traits and personal style of the dreamer. Thus, in late preadolescence, self-participation in REM dreams begins to have sensible personality correlates: individualistic and assertive children dream most often of an active self. Likewise, competitive children with a strong interest in fantasy violence become REM dreamers of fairly frequent self-initiated aggression, while REM dreamers who frequently dream of an angry self character also display considerable hostility during the presleep period. In late preadolescence, because the act of dreaming no longer necessarily reflects the presence or absence of elementary dream-making skills, its product now can be diagnostic of the dreamer's personality or style of life. Everybody—or almost everybody—now has those elementary dream-making skills, so that their *use* depends on factors other than cognitive maturity.

Among those factors are the different paths of traditional sex-role development of girls and boys. Using my data, Eric Trupin (1976) showed that the late preadolescent boys' dreams were more "agentic" (signs of assertiveness, aggression, risk-taking, self-sufficiency, and success-orientation) while girls' dreams were more "communal" (signs of social consciousness, interpersonal orientation, generosity, and receptivity).

Early Adolescent Dreams and Dreaming

You may suspect by now that my focus on the good organization and integration of REM dream phenomena in late pre-adolescence (ages 11 to 13) presages some adolescent clouds on the horizon. Actually, as can be illustrated by some of Emily's non-REM reports, these clouds already cast some shadow at ages 11 to 13. During those years Emily started to have some non-narrative non-REM reports, images of isolated objects outside the context of any kind of imagined story. One index of the possibility of such imagery occurring in *REM* sleep as well is the frequency of reports with vague or absent settings. At ages 11 to 13, such reports were given most often by children who were cognitively talented, conscientious, and responsible. Our brief tour of early adolescent (ages 13 to 15) REM dreaming begins with the observation that the frequency of such vague or settingless reports increases significantly, and this type of dream has the same kind of visual-spatial waking correlates (including Block Design) that predicted new dream skills in the younger study group from ages 5 to 9.

As well as having non-REM reports of objects without backgrounds, Emily had a number of *REM* dreams at ages 13 to 15 that had only slightly more narrative context than those non-REM reports: a piece of candy is thrown out in a street, and she picks it up; she is dishing water out of a well with a ladle; she is looking at her tonsils in the mirror; she and her friend are looking at a green-tipped pen; she is dragging around a great big bow made of ribbon (the Appendix contains complete accounts of Emily's REM-sleep dreams). The settings in these fragments, if any, are implied more than portrayed. The focus, even if someone else is present, is not on social interaction.

These reports come from a child whose REM reports two years earlier illustrated the more general high point of early adolescence in the representation of physical activity and pleasurable social interaction. Now her reports illustrate a general breakdown of this earlier dreaming achievement, as the narrative imperative, the interpersonal focus, and the kinematic versatility of preadolescent dreaming seemingly lose some of their force. I say "some," because it isn't the case that most early adolescent dreams are like the dreams I've just cited—most REM dreams still have settings and locomotion and interaction. It's just that, in early adolescence, you start seeing some REM dreams that lack these expected elements.

What is going on here? Descriptively, the following changes occur in REM dreams between ages 11 to 13 and 13 to 15: there is less concrete portrayal of physical activity (manual acts and locomotion); there is less social interaction; there is more character and setting "distortion" (relative incidence of unknown or unfamiliar persons and places). In thinking about *why* "good-form" dreaming might be breaking down in early adolescence, two major hypotheses come to mind.

Old-style dream theories would say that dreaming primarily reflects the feeling side of our existence, and since adolescence introduces new problems relating to sexuality and personal identity, dreaming would be peculiarly vulnerable to the caprices of adolescent development. On this account, all those dreams Emily was having about impersonal objects really reflected curiosity about her own body parts or those of the opposite sex. In fact, overt references to body states—primarily hunger and fatigue—*decreased* significantly at the onset of adolescence, and sexual imagery was highly infrequent, appearing in 1% of boys' dreams and in 3% of girls' dreams. Lest you imagine that these very few instances of "sexual" imagery refer to dream orgies, I point out that our scoring system had an extraordinarily broad definition of sexual content: "any dream where a boy treats a girl specifically as a girl rather than as an indiscriminate other, and vice-versa" (Foulkes & Shepherd, 1971, p. 15).

Now it is true that some of Emily's dreams could be read as being expressively *symbolic* of concerns about the workings of the female and male sexual apparatus. But I see no way in which the existence of such symbolism could be either confirmed or denied, making it of little real scientific interest. But suppose that we grant that the symbolism is there. Even then, the data would not necessarily imply that body symbolism is forced on adolescent dream life by burgeoning sexual impulses; rather, they might only indicate that some adolescents are able to express symbolically their newfound curiosity about sexuality in dream imagery.

The other hypothesis about what is happening in early adolescent dreaming, one to which this book may have sensitized you, is that dreaming reflects cognitive status, and that the new stage on which adolescent dreaming is being played has been altered by the further cognitive maturation that accompanies adolescence. If the first hypothesis trades on the stereotype of the unruly adolescent, this one points to the newly idealistic adolescent, who now can abstract causes and ideals out of the concrete commerce of social life, and to the "hypothetical-minded" adolescent, who no longer takes life as it comes but instead asks, "But, what if . . . ?"

In psychological theory, this new set of abstract cognitive abilities is sometimes called "formal operational reasoning." The term comes from Jean Piaget (see Flavell, 1963; Gruber & Vonèche, 1977), and its referents, like the rest of Piaget's theory, have been subjected to much criticism by American developmental psychologists, who don't think reasoning develops in stages and who don't believe younger children's cognitive talents are as limited as Piaget thought they were. But the persisting general appeal of Piaget's approach is that it addressed a phenomenon and tried to explain it. There *is* something qualitatively different about adolescent thought. It isn't just the body that changes fundamentally in adolescence in North American middle-class society; it's also the mind. Maybe dreams reflect the newfound possibility of representation that no longer needs to be so concrete and literal, and the adolescent's shift from pure pragmatics to the possibility of theorizing.

One way to test these competing hypotheses would be to correlate waking variables with dream phenomena in early adolescence. Who is on the cutting edge of dream changes at adolescence? Is it the children with the most advanced physical maturation? The children with the most problems of adjustment? Or the brightest children? We have already seen that it is the brightest children who have more of the settingless or vague-setting dreams, and these children are bright in the same visual-spatial competencies that guided dream construction at its outset and in its early development. Likewise, distortion of characters and distortion of settings (which were significantly interrelated) were not predicted by personality dysfunction, but did have some correlates in good visual-spatial reasoning.

After the apex of self-representation had been reached at ages 11 to 13, there were significant *decreases* in such representation at ages 13 to 15. Locomotor activity by the self and prosocial activity initiated by the self had been the major "self" forms of motor activity and of social interaction, respectively, in preadolescence; both declined significantly in early adolescence. Correlated with the retention of self-participation in early adolescent dreams was a visual-spatial package, including Block Design. Frequent dreamers of other characters' activities, by contrast, were relatively poor in visual-spatial skill. This pattern strongly suggests that early adolescents have difficulties in representing active participation of the self character in dream events. Although such participation happens less often, when it is achieved, it happens most often for children with good dream-making skills.

What could the new problem be? I don't know for certain, but I will hazard a guess, based on waking observations that adolescents are increasingly able to step back from themselves, to think about an interactive situation not as they do or the other party does, but as some third, disinterested person might. In dreaming, what this might mean is the development of double self-reference: you, as observer, now can see you, as actor, doing things. In such a framework, imagining self-locomotion, for instance, now poses new representational difficulties: one, but not both, of the dream selves must be subject to visual-spatial displacement. And the finding of the longitudinal study at ages 13 to 15 was that self-locomotion was dreamed relatively most often by children with high visual-spatial skills (including both raw scores and increases in Block Design).

Obviously, more focused research is needed to tell the full story of early adolescent dreaming. At present, I think it is fair to say that the evidence suggests that the dream changes in self representation found in the longitudinal study from late preadolescence to early adolescence do not stem from problems of psychosocial or psychosexual adjustment. Rather, they seem to suggest new possibilities of cognitive self-representation, creating new hurdles in dream construction that are first and best passed by visually-spatially talented children.

It is interesting that the correlates of self-locomotion and of unarticulated-setting dreams both include visual-spatial measures such as Block Design. This indicates that reduced activity of the self character in adolescent dreams is not a by-product of the increase in isolated-object dreaming. Had that been the case, for instance, children not able to dream isolated objects would be limited to more familiar dream forms, such as self-involved dream narratives, and the two dream classes would have contrasting cognitive correlates. As it is, the more likely situation seems to be that increases in formal or abstract thinking in early adolescence facilitate both a new form of narrative realization—double self-reference—and the possibility of escaping entirely or almost entirely from the narrative imperative.

Some developments at ages 13 to 15 were continuous with earlier trends. For example, cognition within the dream by dream characters reached its maximum in our longitudinal series (despite the corresponding decline in overt physical activity), appearing in roughly one REM dream out of every four. Feelings, interestingly enough, actually decreased slightly. The ascription of thoughts and of feelings to dream characters had positive cognitive correlates, visual-spatial ones in the case of feelings. Even in the supposed emotional turmoil of adolescence, cognitive ability rather than waking adjustment seemed to be the strongest determinant of having dreams with emotional content.

During early adolescence, with both REM report and word-count measures stabilized, the two were strongly intercorrelated. Report rate had cognitive correlates, however, while word count did not. At no age level that we studied, from ages 3 to 15, did Block Design predict REM word counts, whereas that test was a strong predictor of both REM recall and new achievements in the constructional competence of dreams. At ages 13 to 15, REM word counts were longer for children of higher social class backgrounds with good social skills. Thus (with the possible exception of ages 7 to 9), REM word count—how much dream is reported when it is remembered at all—probably better reflects the sort of middle-class socialization that makes the child a cooperative research subject, while REM report rate, which has been the prime focus of my account of children's dreaming, is a more likely reflection of the actual presence of dream experience during REM sleep.

Journey's End

At the end of my presentation of the research findings of the longitudinal and the cross-sectional studies of children's dreaming, are any or many of these findings "startling," as I promised in the Introduction? If you are among those who have not encountered them before, I'm sure that at least some of them are. The research data portray a course of dream development which, once it is pointed out to us, makes sense; if it hadn't been pointed out, we probably never would have guessed.

This is why some of us do research in psychology, to make discoveries that challenge prior wisdom and, in the process, make us more knowledgeable. We do not set out deliberately to challenge common sense, which, after all, has much to recommend it. But common sense leaves us with puzzles such as dreaming, which we can't understand. If research makes these puzzles more comprehensible, it's worth the trouble, and the expense, because understanding who we are is the most important understanding of all. In the two closing chapters I suggest ways in which the research on children's dreaming reviewed here may advance, first, our understanding of dreaming, and next, our understanding of the growth of uniquely human aspects of mind and self.

7

~

Dreaming

Its Development

The popular belief is that young children and infants dream more or less the same way that we do—even if, necessarily, about different things. Underlying this belief that dreaming is a given in human nature is the assumption that if one can see reality, one ought also be able to "see" imagined realities. I argue that dreaming is not like seeing, that its composition involves high-level thought processes rather than automatic perceptual ones. The evidence of the preceding three chapters on children's sleep-laboratory dream reports has provided strong confirmation of this position.

We now see that dreaming is not a "given" in human nature. Dreaming develops in predictable stages, and over a longer time span and far later in childhood than we may have imagined. The longitudinal study of children's dreaming identified the stages, and the cross-sectional study replicated the heart of this pattern: to begin with, static imaging; followed by kinematic imagery; and then by active participation in dream events by the self character, the last two typically occurring only sometime after age 7.

But these two studies have done something far more than merely chart the early development of human dreaming. They have furthered our understanding of dreaming itself. Specifically, they have shown us, in conjunction with the neuropsychological studies identifying dreaming with waking imaging, what sort of process dreaming is and what sort of process it isn't. In this regard, they provide the first really new insight into dreaming since the discovery in the 1950s of REM sleep, and the demonstration of its relation to particularly memorable dreaming.

We now see that dreaming *is* a very high-level cognitive process that has skill prerequisites lacking in infancy and which unfold slowly in the preschool and early primary-school years. We now know that dreaming *is not* an elementary and automatically engaged adjunct of waking perceptual processes, and that it cannot, therefore, be imagined to be present in every creature whose waking behavior is visually (or otherwise sensorially) guided. To dream, it isn't enough to be able to *see*. You have to be able to *think* in a certain way. Specifically, you have to be able, in your mind's eye, to simulate, at first momentarily and later in more extended episodes, a conscious reality that is not supported by current sense data and that you've never even experienced before.

Now, the question might be raised whether this notion of dreaming, the imaginal simulation of a novel "reality" in the absence of supporting sense data (which certainly embraces our adult notion of what a dream is), exhausts the possible forms of sleep mentation that could occur in very young children or other animals. Maybe, for instance, infants and animals have nonreflective forms of sensation during sleep not at all like our dreaming, but still "occurring involuntarily in the mind during . . . sleep" (see the dictionary definition cited earlier).

I have taken "in the mind" to mean consciously experienced, and in that sense I don't think these hypothetical nonreflective sensations in sleep could qualify as dreaming in any manner that would be at all faithful either to everyday linguistic usage or to the pursuit of scientific psychological inquiry. There is, of course, the uncomfortable fact that such sensations must remain forever hypothetical, for we have no way of knowing whether or when they might actually exist.

Even supposing that in-sleep "sensations" or perceptions *were* the object of conscious reflection, would they be dreams? As a graduate student, I remember collecting a report following awakening from an unbroken stretch of non-REM sleep in which the sleeper claimed to have been listening to the sound of plumbing pipes down the hall from his bedroom. I, too, presumably awake next door, had heard the same pipes, which during the 1950s in Abbott Hall at the University of Chicago were in fact periodically prone to "act up" at odd times of the night. Would we want to say, in this case, that the person had dreamed of hearing pipes, or that he had merely heard them? The latter, I think, is the far more plausible choice. This indicates that not even all *conscious* mental activity during sleep immediately qualifies as dreaming; rather, dreaming inherently implies some imaginal irreality, taken to be real.

The same sort of definitional quandary arose in the early study of adult non-REM mentation, when some reports ("I was thinking about this phone call I got from home tonight. . . . I was rehearsing [my parents'] conversation in my mind" [Foulkes, 1962, p. 21]) were designated "thinking" rather than "dreaming." Evidently, there is something about totally reality-grounded conscious mentation occurring during sleep that makes us reluctant to consider it dreaming. Such mentation certainly would not call for a novel explanatory framework in scientific psychology, in the way that dreams do.

What my data suggest, then, is that the kind of conscious cognition that makes the dreaming form of ideation possible is, if generally present at all, very rudimentary in the preschool period, and only develops into full form between the ages 5 to 9. As with any high-level cognitive competency, this kind of thinking does not turn itself on all at once. During sleep, it appears by predictable stages, and even within stages, its early manifestation seems to be sporadic, as shown by the low report rates on REM awakenings before age 9.

I've also shown that the increasing ability to use sleep periods for the exercise of dream-making skills is itself a predictable process. This process begins in late-night REM sleep, then later extends to earlier and deeper REM sleep periods as well as to late-night non-REM sleep, and finally appears in earlier and deeper non-REM sleep periods. The lawful, and expected direction of this growth in dream-reporting suggests an underlying reality of growing skills in dream-making.

You could still argue, of course, that this is merely a predictable pattern by which children become aware of dreaming, which is going on most or all the time during REM sleep and sometimes during non-REM sleep as well. But it seems strange to have a slowly developing awareness focused on an underlying process that is, by comparison, amazingly precocious. If awareness is such a slow learner, how did dreaming get to be so smart so fast? Why and how should dreaming be an exception to the rule that no high-level cognitive process, which is what the independent adult neuropsychological data show dreaming to be, arrives both very early and fully formed?

One counterproposal to the developmental link of cognition and dreaming is that maybe dream imagery is present all along, even in infancy, but children aren't yet consciously aware of it. Well, if there is imagery, there *has* to be conscious awareness, because you have to be consciously aware of something for it to be "imagery." And, if there are supposed to be narrative simulations of which the person is not consciously aware, then they can't be "dreaming," since dreaming necessarily implies consciousness (awareness of a mental state). The heart of the dreaming phenomenon is that we consciously experience as reality events that aren't real.

Whatever else is hypothetically proposed to be going on outside consciousness cannot be dreaming. And if this hypothetical dream-making is going on at so high a level below conscious awareness, how is it that, when the child first "simply" becomes aware of dreaming, the object of that awareness seems to be as simple as the awareness? Why is the content of the child's first report so puny, if the dream-making itself is so grand? Is it just a matter of inadequacies of language and attention in reporting? I don't think so. It is certainly curious, moreover, that the 2- or 3-year-old is quite capable of reporting to us in waking life that the "doggie runned" but doesn't seem to be able to report any running doggies on REM-sleep awakenings.

As I've shown, the cognitive correlates of relatively high rates of dream reporting on REM (and non-REM) awakenings also don't support the alternate scenario of complex dreaming and slow awareness in early and middle childhood. Children who report dreams often generally *don't* have better memories, vocabularies, or descriptive skills than do their low-reporting peers. Where they are different is in possessing certain visual-spatial skills that are more plausibly involved in creating dreams than in remembering and describing them.

Then, too, there is the evidence from adolescents (Foulkes, 1982a) and adults (Butler & Watson, 1985) with no demonstrated impairments in age-appropriate memory or verbal skill but lacking these particular visual-spatial skills, who seem to dream during REM sleep either not at all or not very often. For them, it surely can't be just a matter of poor remembering or describing; it has to be a deficit in dream-*making*.

If consciousness of a mental process, rather than some hypothetical nonconscious process continuously under way during sleep, is the key element of what we call dreaming, then concerns about the possibility of great discrepancies between dreaming and remembering dreaming in early childhood seem quite ill-conceived. It is the same awareness that I have of events while dreaming that makes it possible for me later, on awakening, to remember my dream.

In terms of the example given in the first chapter, about driving a car, it is because I noticed and tried to identify an object in the street ahead of me that I was later able to remember this episode and tell a friend about it. And it is precisely because I was preoccupied with something else, and earlier literally had not consciously attended to my route, that when I snapped out of my "brown study," I could not even remember having driven for some distance over that route or what I might have encountered along the way. Fortunately (for me and for other drivers), I can drive without accident when I drive without awareness. But without awareness of events as they happened, I cannot remember those events. The same holds for the development of dreaming: since dreaming requires awareness, it also, from its first occurrence, is susceptible to later recall. It is simply not plausible to propose that dream occurrence greatly predates and exceeds dream recall.

I should stress here that although awareness is a necessary condition for subsequent conscious recollection of events, it clearly is not a sufficient one. When considering whether an event later will prove to be susceptible of such recollection, it is important to determine how much and what kind of awareness accompanied it. Our awareness during much of dreaming seems relatively passive and literally accepting. We generally do not question, during the dream itself, the plausibility of its unfolding events. We understand what is happening, but we most often don't relate that to the larger context of our current life situation and our overall world knowledge. Put another way, we aren't doing much of the kind of active *encoding* of information that would facilitate later recollection.

It also is misleading to consider dream "events" as if they were just like waking events. Dream events are actively created by our mind much as are waking recollections. When considering why dreams seem so much more easily forgotten than waking events, we should make the appropriate comparison not with the waking event itself but with its waking recollection. When our mind is organized in a recollective mode, it generally is not organized to *encode* information for subsequent recollection; it is organized, rather, to *retrieve* information (Tulving, 1983; Foulkes, 1985, pp. 77–87).

Its Conditions and Its Creativity

Dreaming often is viewed as a form, and one of the prime forms, of human creativity. Is dreaming creative, and, if so, does it have anything to tell us about creativity more generally? We've seen how, from the very outset, dreaming *is* creative, that it doesn't just rehash or anticipate waking life but instead produces novel organizations of experience. Almost always, even for the youngest child who can dream, the dream creates situations or events that never before have been encountered in just that form. Dreaming that you are asleep in a bathtub, the very first REM dream report collected from Dean in the longitudinal study (see the Appendix), is creative in just this way. Granted, this isn't Rembrandt- or Shakespeare-style creativity. But it's a reasonable entree into the world of adult dreaming, whose products typically are novel—never before encountered just this way—but also quite mundane and realistic, rather than creative in the way often elaborated in novels and films (Snyder, 1970; Foulkes, 1985). It seems difficult to reconcile the novelty of dreams with their mundane realism. Yet this provides the key to understanding the very nature of dreaming.

As I've indicated, dreaming is not limited to REM sleep. It also clearly occurs during much non-REM sleep and during the transition from wakefulness to sleep. Dreaming even has been observed, if generally momentarily, in relaxed wakefulness, when people let their minds "go" or "wander" (Foulkes & Scott, 1973; Foulkes & Fleisher, 1975). The occurrence of dreaming in ordinary non-REM sleep, at sleep onset, and in relaxed wakefulness has been repeatedly documented and is now generally accepted. This means that conditions or mechanisms unique to REM sleep cannot explain dreaming (compare Hobson, 1988).

Basically, there are three conditions required for dreaming: persisting cortical (physiological) and cognitive (psychological) activation; occlusion or dampening of external stimulation; and—the key—relinquishing voluntary self-control of ideation. The cortical and cognitive activation means that *some kind* of conscious ideation will be experienced; the other two conditions dictate the dreamlike form of that ideation.

The two great regulators of the waking mind that keep our ideation on track and prevent constant, incessant dreaming are the world and the self. By the world I mean the patterned stimulation provided by both physical and social reality. Reality stimulation is a great organizer and regulator of our mental life. We may believe that we think whatever we want, but our mental activity is under a great degree of control by where we are and who we are with. In sleep, we lose the outer world. We shut our eyes, we turn off the lights, we try to reduce sound stimulation to some low or repetitious level. But the world is lost to us not only as a result of our voluntary activity in seeking to reduce external stimulation, but also as a result of sleep mechanisms in the brain that actively shut down the processing of external stimulation impinging upon it. Rechtschaffen and Foulkes (1965) showed that, even if the eyes are kept "open" during sleep, the sleepers neither recognize nor dream about stimuli presented to them.

We also, at sleep onset, lose our self (Foulkes & Vogel, 1965; Vogel, Foulkes, & Trosman, 1966). We relinquish voluntary control of our ideation. We lose our sense of where we are, and, in a very real sense, of who we are. Our subsequent dream experience is not continuous with our presleep conscious ideation, and we don't, during dreaming, have access to the same range of personal history that we had just before going off to sleep. As any insomniac can attest, failure to be able to let go of self-awareness and self-control prevents sleep from happening. And so, one price of achieving sleep is losing the self that voluntarily, intentionally, regulates our waking mind. It is not just the world that helps us to organize our waking thought, but also our conscious intentions about how we want to address that world. And even when we are still physiologically awake, if we relinquish that sort of voluntary control of our ideation, we dream (Foulkes & Scott, 1973; Foulkes & Fleisher, 1975).

The persistent mental activation that underlies dreaming must therefore be without intrinsic direction. Neither world nor self harnesses that activation to some particular purpose or goal. The activation is widespread, and it is dissociated, in the sense that different units of representation of memory and knowledge are active despite their lack of an everyday relation to one another or to the pursuit of some common goal. There is no longer a self to suppress irrelevant activation, as happens when we are working on some problem in waking life, because there is no longer an intention that makes something relevant or irrelevant. As we've seen, from the outset of dream reporting, children's dreams do have the property of portraying together representations of experience or knowledge that ordinarily don't fit together in waking life (and presumably aren't stored or filed together in memory). Dreams are novel.

But they also are organized, and according to the best sleep-laboratory evidence, very well organized indeed (Foulkes, 1985). Momentarily, there is coherent imagery, rather than some kind of phantasmagorical jumble. Sequentially, there is a story or narrative that generally carries characters, setting, and events along a coherent course across time (Foulkes & Schmidt, 1983). These forms of dream organization are operations of consciousness. Dreaming *is* the form assumed by consciousness under the three conditions described above. Thus dreaming is not a "special" process, unique to sleep. Dreaming is, rather, what happens when consciousness, the very same as waking consciousness, operates under the three conditions outlined above.

To understand this, let us think for a moment about waking consciousness. From a cognitive-psychological perspective, consciousness is a high-level system for selecting and organizing information. It is selective, because there are so many things of which, at any moment, we *could* be conscious, but so few of which we *are*. The system we call consciousness has evolved for organisms such as ourselves, whose behavior is not predetermined but involves choice. I know what the moth is going to do when I turn on the light; I don't know what I'm going to do. Although consciousness does not always dictate action—I may decide consciously that I'm going to do something, but not do it—it clearly is oriented toward presenting a summation of currently available information upon which intelligent action choices might be made.

In this regard, waking consciousness seems to operate under at least two constraints. First, it must *faithfully* represent the current situation. Second, it must *coherently* represent the current situation. Consciousness would not have evolved if it did not promote realistic responses to situations. Thus it must give an accurate, if necessarily selective, account of what's "out there." But it would be maladaptive as well if consciousness reflected every small inconsistency or shift in informational input. We respond more efficiently to a "big picture" than to a hopelessly qualified or internally inconsistent pattern of information. Consistency also is important over time. Although the world is in constant flux, it would drive us crazy to have to keep up with that. We prefer, other things being equal, to see the future as a sensible continuation of the present. When inputs become really different, then (maybe) we'll make a change, but the system's bias is to continuity over time just as it is to consistency of the moment.

Now, imagine that this daytime system for analysis and synthesis of information is put to work during REM sleep (or in any of the other states in which dreaming is observed). It wants to give a realistic portrayal of currently available information—of the numerous seemingly unrelated or only partly related units of memory and knowledge then active. To do so invariably involves novelty, since these items do not fit together by the standards of waking experience. But it also wants to give a coherent portrayal of what it finds, and so the ensuing, selective form of its portrayal of novelty is coherent imaging, and, over time, coherent narratizing.

Steering between the twin constraints of faithfulness and coherence must be more difficult without the world and self to organize ideation. The atypical occurrence of bizarreness of image *form* in representatively sampled REM dreams indicates that such a course is not always successfully navigated. But the more general observation is that, despite its variegated and shifting source material in mnemonic activation, dreaming makes very good sense of disparate ingredients. And, of course, what we take to be errors in image *content*—putting together in coherent imagery things that don't belong to-gether—reflects the laudable goal that consciousness ought faithfully to reflect what it encounters.

Thus when we understand that dreaming is the form taken by consciousness during sleep (and at other times as well), when we understand what consciousness more generally is and does, and when we understand the nature of the information that dreaming must operate upon, we understand dreaming. Dreaming is the operation of typical waking consciousness in the atypical conditions of sleep or wakefulness in the absence of self.

These conditions are atypical, at least by waking standards, because they include the simultaneous activation of units of memory and knowledge whose referents need not be closely related in waking experience and whose neural representations in the brain presumably might not necessarily be closely con-nected either. Beside the theoretical deduction that, lacking effective integration by world and self, the mind would be ac-tive in a more variegated and diffuse way, we also have empiri-cal evidence that this is in fact the case.

First, of course, there is the appearance in dream imagery it-self of incongruent elements. Why is Uncle Harry, who lives in Florida, suddenly a dream co-worker of a friend of mine, whom he's never met or even heard of? A second line of evi-dence comes from the use of free association in clinical inter-views with patients of therapists who use some form of dream analysis. The typical finding is that the dream itself is much more unified than the associations given to it (Foulkes, 1985). The dream generally is a fairly coherent story, circumscribed in space, time, and subject matter. The associations, on the other hand, most likely span both the lifetime of the dreamer and the many areas of his or her current interest and involvement. Since the associations are supposed to index possible sources of the dream, these data suggest that the dream's sources are diffuse and variegated.

More direct evidence has come from recent sleep-laboratory studies in which dreamers are asked, after having reported their dreams, where they think the dream imagery might have come from, that is, what its sources might have been (Cavallero & Cicogna, 1993). Once again, the dream's sources, as identified by the dreamer, are far more diverse and diffuse than is the dream itself.

But it is also possible to overstate the diversity and diffuseness of the dream's sources. These sources must after all lie in the memories and knowledge of the dreamer: it is where the dream finds its raw material. We know that our representation of discrete memories and general knowledge is itself organized and meaningfully interrelated; a large part of the effort of the cognitive branch of psychology has gone into validating and describing that organization. Thus, although several units of memory and knowledge may be activated during dreaming, these units themselves are organized and interrelated such that activation spreads among them in meaningful ways. So it would be erroneous to think of the sources of the dream as being random, because that's neither how we represent nor how we store the information from which dreams are made.

The most prevalent theory currently being popularized about dreaming, however, states that the sources of dreaming lie in "chaotic signals originating in the brainstem" (Rittenhouse, Stickgold, & Hobson, 1994, p. 112; see also Hobson, 1988). Although these authors' later view is that there are cortical associative constraints imposed on brainstem inputs that lead to some dream coherence, their original notion of randomness seems to have been the source of their theory's initial impact and to be the basis of its continuing attraction. The randomness notion leads to the following description of REM dreaming: "the mind becomes formally psychotic. Wild and bizarre delusions are fed by visual and auditory hallucinations. . . . The mind becomes hyperemotional, alternately terrified and ecstatic. Profound anxiety alternates with a sense of omnipotent grandiosity" (Stickgold & Hobson, 1994, pp. 141–2).

This sketch of dream phenomenology sounds nothing like my account of Dream A of adults and nothing like my data on the developing Dream A of children. It probably doesn't even sound like most persons' idea of their Dream B. But it does dramatize the idea of the randomness of an out-of-control dream process.

Now the original idea of chaotic brainstem dream sources rests on the empirical observation that cortical and cognitive activation are initiated by the brainstem. But Hobson and McCarley (1977) further proposed that the informational sources of dreams come from that same level, and hence are both random and meaningless.

But, modifying an analogy by an early critic of this theory, Gerald Vogel (1978), suppose that there's a primitive mechanism in the cellar of a house that periodically turns on the lights and rouses the creatures living upstairs. What happens next depends entirely on the properties and traits of the creatures at the upper levels (it is to this point that Rittenhouse, Stickgold, and Hobson [1994] now make some small concession). These creatures are not being guided at a distance from below, in the way that some psychotics believe their thoughts are under external control.

In wakefulness, cortical arousal also is initiated by the brainstem, but no one, I suppose, imagines that the form or substance of waking conscious ideation is determined by the brainstem. Why, then, should we suppose this to be the case during sleep? There is no physiological evidence that REM and waking cortical arousal are in any important respect functionally different from one another (Steriade, 1996). There also is absolutely no independent evidence that subcortical neural arousal of the cortex is accompanied by a transfer of psychological information capable of either influencing or reaching conscious representation. Thus, in general, we must assume that it is the properties of the aroused cortical representational networks rather than those of the subcortical arousers that determine the content of conscious ideation. Wholly consistent with this position, and in direct refutation of Hobson's position, is the recent review by Solms (1997) showing that deep brainstem lesions generally are not accompanied by cessation of dream experience, while such cessation does follow certain cortical lesions, despite the preservation of brainstem-initiated REM sleep.

The Hobson group's reductionist theory of dream generation stands in opposition to the purely psychological theories. In each case, the goal is an explanation of dreaming: why does it happen in the first place, and what kind of process is it? The reductionist proposes that for each ordinary or puzzling feature of conscious dreaming (A, B, C, D, etc.) there is or must be one or more underlying physiological correlates (a, b, c, d, etc.), such that, when we understand the temporal course of activation, inhibition, facilitation, and so on among the physiological correlates, we will have explained dreaming. This presupposes, of course, that correlation will evidence causation, a generally risky presupposition.

And, although it is a matter of faith (!) in the neurosciences that reductionism in the sense of showing one-to-one (or maybe, more messily, one-to-many) correlations between mental experiences and brain events is possible, we cannot be sure that that is the case until it is exhaustively and conclusively demonstrated. That is unlikely to happen within the lifetime of any reader, however precocious, of this book. Until then, and working toward that possibility, the neuroscientist keeps looking at data collected within the limits of concurrent technical feasibility.

In the meantime, however, and also even in the long run should reductionism somehow succeed, there also must be a place for independent psychological study of phenomena such as dreaming. Psychophysiological correlation must involve equally precise categorizations of physiological events and of the psychological processes or experiences which they purport to explain. The latter domain is that of experimental psychology. And let us suppose that reductionism has somehow succeeded in establishing the relevant correlations between mind and brain for dreaming, and also that it has somehow succeeded in showing that it is the brain that "causes" its mind correlate. Is psychology now irrelevant? Only if you think, as I happen not to, that one can explain dreaming by neuro-humoral secretion patterns or distributions of fast wave activity in certain subcortical centers and cortical areas, without indicating the psychological processes or events that these index, as, for example, activating certain memory systems and inhibiting others, facilitating imaginal processing, and accessing imaginally relevant contextual information. That is, the ultimate form of a dream explanation must be at the level A, B, C, D, which is the psychological level.

And so, if the neurosciences have not yet, for technical reasons that may or may not prove insurmountable, begun to amass data relevant to their side of the psychophysiological equation for dreaming, and if there is, in any event, independent merit for the more immediately practicable psychological approach, that is where, at present and for the foreseeable future, the richest harvests will be made of dream-relevant knowledge.

It is at this level, for instance, that we can find additional evidence of both the diffuseness/unpredictability of the dream's sources and of their organization and meaningfulness. In a recent study (Roussy, Camirand, Foulkes, De Koninck, Loftis, & Kerr, 1996), female college students identified, before they went to sleep, either their most prominent current concerns and worries or their most immediately salient unprompted thoughts. They were awakened shortly after the start of their first REM sleep episode. Judges then tried to match, either across nights for an individual dreamer or across dreamers, the particular presleep ideation that went with (occurred on the same session as) each dream. They were not generally successful in doing so. Thus, it cannot be predicted, from what is on a person's mind just before she falls asleep, what she will be dreaming about later.

But it also was noted that the topics of the dreams and the presleep ideation came from a common pool. Specifically, both the presleep ideation and the dreams most often referred to such areas of the students' lives as academics, family, friends, travel and other plans, jobs, living arrangements, and so forth. Thus although the judges could not predict from the presleep ideation *which* current concern would be represented in later REM dream imagery, invariably *some* such concern was portrayed in it.

Whatever intuitive appeal attaches to the idea that the dream's sources are random derives, I think, from the unpredictability of our dreams. We can't tell, from night to night, what we will dream about and whether some current concern will or will not be reflected in our dream. But such unpredictability does not imply that our dreams are generated randomly or that their sources are meaningless. Our dreams are stimulated by a finite pool of organized and meaningful areas of concern or interest in our lives and minds. That the agenda by which particular sources are selected from this pool differs for waking and dreaming ideation does not make these sources any bit less organized and meaningful. And that the agenda is different should not be surprising, given the presence of voluntary self regulation in one instance and its absence in the other.

We came into this account of what dreaming is and does by way of a question about its creativity. It is clear that dreaming is creative, both in the sense that it produces novel configurations of our memories and knowledge in its imagery, and in the sense that its organization of its diverse sources is exceptionally well accomplished. But the creativity of dreaming, on my account, is pragmatic and down to earth. There is no suggestion that dreaming plumbs the depths of our soul or arches skyward to eternal truths. Whatever creativity there is in dreaming comes from the fact that consciousness, in some-what difficult circumstances, is just doing its job. The reveren-tial attitude that some students of creativity and many dream theorists betray toward dreaming seems misplaced. We should really be in greater awe of ordinary consciousness.

My account of the pragmatic or everyday creativity of dreaming would seem to be belied by two extremes: the dream that is so disorganized that it makes no coherent sense of its disparate sources, and the dream that is so organized it seems to have given up its usual goal of keeping in touch with those sources. The first extreme is, I think, with one important ex-ception, more a dream stereotype than a dream A fact. That is, creative organization of dream sources is almost invariably found in dreaming, particularly during REM sleep.

The exception is found during a certain stage of dreaming at sleep onset (Vogel, Foulkes, & Trosman, 1966), at which point one or more of the following experiences may occur: de-fects in image formation (seeing part, but not all, of a scene; superimposition of unrelated imagery, such as strawberries superimposed on a train station); discontinuity of thought and image (thinking about one thing while seeing a wholly un-related image); defects in narrative sequence (successive events seem unrelated to one another); wholly unrealistic content (people living inside a chest cavity, for instance). These are *not* general features of our most accomplished and extensive dreams—REM-sleep dreams. That they occur, fleetingly, at sleep onset may reflect the kind of bungling that sometimes happens in relay races: as the organizational baton is passed from wakeful to sleeping ideation, it is momentarily dropped. In view of the massive shifts in cognitive organization required by the passage from wakefulness to sleep, lapses in ideational integration might be expected. Perhaps more surprising is how infrequent and very brief these lapses are, and how quickly ordinary dreamlike organization asserts itself.

The other challenge to my account of the pragmatic creativity of dreaming is the dream that seems to get carried away with itself. It used to be said of a famous news magazine that it never let the facts get in the way of its telling a good story. Likewise, it seems that in some dreams, the narrative becomes detached from its original sources and the dreamer begins to spin a tale whose nature is entirely self-contained. The emerging dream seems entirely narrative-driven and not at all source-driven; reporting what memory units are currently active has been sacrificed in the service of telling a really good story. The frequency of this sort of dream has, like that of the other extreme discussed above, been greatly overestimated, in this case probably because waking memory has flattened the rough edges of the original dream experience while greatly embellishing its storyline. But this kind of dream clearly can and does occur. And when it does, professional dream interpreters pounce upon it as ultimately self-revealing. Jung (1960), for instance, would see these as "big" dreams, in contrast to pragmatically creative, and hopelessly ordinary, "little" dreams.

But all that such dreams may reveal is the narrative capacity and the narrative propensity of the dreamer. Just as we can, awake, get so caught up in a line of daydreaming that we pursue it without regard to anything else, so too, apparently, when we dream we can dream for the sake of having a really good dream without regard to anything else, as if the narrative is now guiding memory activation rather than the more usual reverse case.

Both of the extreme cases under discussion are endpoints on a single continuum of source-integration interaction, the former being all source and the latter all integration, with the most usual case consisting of a mixture of the two. Many dream theorists, however, follow Jung in identifying different kinds of dreams and proposing different mechanisms for each (most notably, Hunt, 1989). I don't see that as either a fruitful way of opening scientific inquiry or as a plausible hypothesis about how dreaming evolved. Dream consciousness presumably began simply, and complexity ensued only as was absolutely necessary, and that's how we should be conducting our studies of dream consciousness.

Its Functions

Evolutionary considerations often raise the question of the function of dreaming—of its *purpose*. At this cosmic and teleological level, all sorts of functions can be, and have been proposed for dreaming (see, for example, Moffitt, Kramer, & Hoffman, 1993), proposals which are rarely constrained by much empirical evidence. I, too, will indulge in some speculation, but not so much from the perspective of the *purpose* of dreaming as from that of its *effect* (Merton, 1957), which is another, and a possibly more fruitful, empirical way of looking at dream function.

What can it mean for ordinary consciousness to be systematically deployed in such difficult circumstances as the diffuse mental activation that characterizes dreaming? For one thing, it surely must be useful for waking consciousness to receive much "off-line" practice in learning to perform these most taxing of informational summaries in a coherent and cohesive way. It is difficult not to believe that this work is adaptive. But it bears repeating that this function only can exist for those who are capable of dreaming and of our kind of consciousness—it certainly has nothing to do with the original but still unknown function of REM sleep.

Thus we reach the unremarkable conclusion that dreaming can have effects only for those organisms that dream, a conclusion that becomes more remarkable when paired with our newfound understanding that those organisms probably only include post-infantile human beings. This means that the effects of dreaming cannot have anything to do with elementary tasks of biological or social adaptation, which have been mastered already by the late preschool years. Given our also newfound understanding that dreaming is a high-level cognitive process, it probably makes the most sense to start thinking about effects within dreaming's own domain: conscious cognition. And if I am right about the close connection between dream and waking consciousness, the question of dream effects becomes, at least in part, a question about the function of consciousness more generally. An interesting corollary is that the more general question might be addressed by comparing children of given ages who either do or do not show certain dream accomplishments, since these may index characteristics of their waking consciousness as well.

Aligning the creative and other achievements of dreaming with waking consciousness also has definite implications for the *purposive* approach to dream function. Why do we dream?

What is the function of dreaming? What, if anything, are dreams good for? For the moment, let me approach these questions just in the context of REM-sleep dreaming.

We think that we *do* have some idea what the function of consciousness is. For the human organism, the stimuli that are faced and the behavioral choices that are available are many and complex. There is, therefore, an adaptive advantage in forming a representation of the conceptual or action field that is most faithful to the information currently available and that remains coherent and consistent over time. You don't always have to act in accord with that representation, but it's there when you need it.

In contrast, we *don't* know what is the function of REM sleep, despite the best efforts of some of our best researchers (Rechtschaffen, Bergmann, Everson, Kushida, & Gilliland, 1989). From its prevalence among almost all mammals and possibly some birds, from its rebound after short-term deprivation, and from the fact that death follows its systematic long-term loss (Kushida, Bergmann, & Rechtschaffen, 1989), we believe that REM sleep *must* have some function, but we can't, as yet, say what that might be. We do know, both from the appearance of REM sleep (phylogenetically *and* ontogenetically) long before there is the possibility of dreaming, and from the fact that human dreaming does not require REM sleep, that the function of REM sleep has nothing to do with dreaming. REM dreaming is the adventitious by-product of the two developments identified above as themselves having functions—consciousness and REM sleep—when they first intersect in human children. Dreaming ensues when activation from downstream—in the brainstem—excites a cortex and mind upstream that have the cognitive capacities necessary for conscious world simulation, without receiving any stimulation from the world outside at that time. And, as we've seen, the activation required from the brainstem does not have to be of a specifically REM variety—it can be the steady, tonic activation of relaxed wakefulness; it can be the decreasing but residually strong activation of sleep onset; or it can be the decreased but still present activation of ordinary non-REM sleep.

Thus there's a strong sense that dreaming occurs when and where it does because it *has* to. Given the activation, given the relinquishment of self control, and given that we have the possibility, no, the imperative, of generating conscious representations of currently active information whether we are awake or asleep, whether we are attending external reality or not, then dreaming has to happen. In a way, my conclusion here is much like my conclusion about the creativity of dreaming: namely, that given the boundary conditions, dreaming has to be creative. Likewise, given the boundary conditions, there has to be dreaming. But in neither case are the boundary conditions there so that the phenomenon can occur: we don't have dissociated mental activation so that we can be creative, and we don't have the capability of conscious symbolic representation so that we can dream. It's just that these phenomena ensue given, respectively, the properties of a mental activation that is not self-directed, and the properties of human consciousness in the face of such activation.

This line of plausible reasoning suggests that we are in error when we ask for, propose, or accept grandiose theories of the function of dreaming. Dreaming isn't so special, after all; it doesn't require theories of the magnitude and complexity most often sought or given. The by-product of two phenomena themselves of great functional significance—internally generated cortical activation (REM or not) and consciousness itself—it is possible that dreaming itself has no special purpose. At any rate, the real functional questions of significance transcend dreaming as such, and, in the case of consciousness, become questions about the function and adaptive value of a phenomenon that presumably has evolved for its role in our waking life. We do not achieve consciousness so that we can dream; we dream because we have achieved consciousness.

8

Consciousness

Infantile Amnesia

Probably the most striking cognitive difference between the preschool years and later life is our inability to remember events from the first few years of our lives. This phenomenon is known technically as "infantile amnesia," although the memory gap extends well past infancy to include the first four or five years of life. Many explanations have been proposed for our inability to recreate the circumstances of early life, but that such explanations keep on coming suggests, correctly, that none has yet penetrated to the heart of the matter. Nor, as Katherine Nelson (1996) has noted, has the phenomenon of infantile amnesia itself had nearly the impact that it should have had on general theories of cognitive development.

Freud (1899) noted the phenomenon of infantile amnesia in his paper entitled "Screen Memories," his name for unreliable memories that seem to, but don't really, come from the first years of our lives. Other keen observers of human experience had earlier identified the phenomenon. Anthony Trollope, for instance, constructed a humorous scene around the concept in his 1859 novel, *The Bertrams* (1993 edition). After having stated that he had never before seen his father, who following his mother's early death "had roamed the world free from all encumbrances (p. 5)," George Bertram explains to the contentious Mr. M'Gabbery:

"I never saw him to remember him. One doesn't count one's acquaintance before seven or eight years of age."

"Your memory must be very bad, then," said Mr. M'Gabbery, "or your childhood's love for your father very slight."

[To make his point, Mr. M'Gabbery goes on to recount a very early childhood "memory," looking at a picture book as he stood by his mother's knee. Determined not to be outdone, George goes on to concoct a still earlier one, to the amusement of the ladies in the party.]

"I must tell you about my memory. I was lying once in my cradle—"

"You don't mean to tell me you remember that?" said M'Gabbery.

"Perfectly, as you do the picture-book. Well, there I was lying, Miss Baker, with my little eyes wide open. It is astonishing how much babies see. . . . I was lying on my back, staring at the mantelpiece, on which my mother had left her key-basket."

"You remember, of course, that it was her key-basket?" said Miss Waddington, with a smile that made M'Gabbery clench his walking-stick in his hand.

"Perfectly; because she always kept her halfpence there also. Well, there was a nursery-girl who used to be about me in those days. I distinctly saw her go to that basket, Miss Baker, and take out a penny; and I then made up my mind that the first use

I would make of my coming speech should be to tell my mother. That, I think, is the furthest point to which my memory carries me."

The ladies laughed heartily, but Mr. M'Gabbery frowned bitterly. "You must have dreamt it," said he. (pp. 86–87)

On first hearing about infantile amnesia, many people object that they *do* have memories from infancy or early childhood. Freud's position was that these seeming memories are invalid "screens" that serve to keep us from remembering the really significant events of early life, events that have to do with sexuality, broadly construed. While there is reason to doubt the specifics of Freud's explanation, his suspicion, like that of the ladies in *The Bertrams,* of apparent reminiscence of life's first years seems better founded.

In Chapter 4 I mentioned a vivid "recollection" by Jean Piaget of his own kidnapping. This alleged memory had all of the convincingness of a true memory, but it was false. The event recollected never happened. Its source was a story concocted by his nurse to conceal a romantic liaison and justify the fact that she had not constantly attended her young charge (Piaget, 1962, pp. 187n–188n). This incident convinced Piaget that not every memory, no matter how real or convincing it may seem, is genuine, and it suggested to him that very early memories are most likely to be false ones.

Now, let's be clear about what sort of memory we're talking about here. It's not the kind of memory that allows the child, on going to the shore two years running, to remember that there's a miniature golf course across from the jetty. It doesn't depend on the stimulation of a recurrent setting. It's not even the kind of memory that allows the child to talk about some earlier life event when someone asks about it. That kind of memory can be purely verbal, and is subject to crafting by parents who hope to help the child develop a sense of a personal past by talking about it. The kind of memory to which the infantile amnesia refers is what Endel Tulving (1983) has called *conscious episodic recollection*, the conscious recreation of discrete episodes in our waking lives.

"Re-creation" is a key term here. Contrary to popular theory and to some neurobiological speculation, there is no evidence that we have memory files for each and every one of our experiences, and that remembering is simply accessing intact files from storage, like pulling an old movie off of the shelf. Conscious episodic recollections are momentary constructions out of information left behind by past experiences, as also guided by information acquired subsequent to the event in question (which is why on-the-spot reporting is superior to later recollection). These conscious recollections are actively created, not passively retrieved.

Cognitively, they have the same status as dream images— they simulate reality purely from information currently available in the cognitive system. They are unlike dream images only in that they are, on occasion at least, purposefully generated, and in that the information currently available is much more circumscribed and focused. These are important differences, of course, but they should not blind us to the essential similarity of the mental processing in each case.

Which is why the general absence and/or the very limited representational quality of dreaming until age 5 or so puts a new spin on thinking about infantile amnesia. Infantile amnesia is the inability to consciously recreate episodes from the first few years of life, and the period of its sway coincides with the general absence and/or puniness of dream generation. In each case, there is a deficit of consciousness, specifically an inability to simulate reality purely from information available in the cognitive system.

In its waking guise, this inability suggests that the actual experience of events is different in the earliest years of life. Infantile amnesia is puzzling to the degree that one imagines that young children are experiencing events just as older children and adults do. If that is the case, then why can't we consciously remember them as we do the events of later years? But suppose that early childhood events are not experienced the way that we experience later ones. Suppose that children's experience of events is more like my driving the route without awareness than like my looking to see just what object lies in the road ahead. Then our failure to recall events consciously from the first few years of life is consistent with my failure to recall consciously the details of my driving route. To be recalled consciously, an event must first be experienced consciously. Otherwise, the information of the event permitting later recollection is simply not registered.

Consciousness Develops

In the preceding chapter, I hypothesized that dreaming is simply the operation of consciousness during sleep (and some other states), and I observed that dreaming develops more slowly and later than is generally believed. To this I now add the hypothesis that consciousness develops, and that it does so more slowly and later than is generally believed. The often noted "shift" in waking cognition from ages 5 to 7 (White, 1965; Sameroff & Haith, 1996) involves, on this new hypothesis, the development of the possibility of coding, or of recoding, knowledge in consciously accessible form. Until age 5 or so, there is little or no such coding, and therefore no possibility of conscious episodic recollection. It is not that children aren't learning from experience, just that what they've learned and what they know are not yet consciously accessible as episodic recollections.

This view, derived from dream data, of consciousness as a developing phenomenon is not widely accepted by American developmental psychologists. They, perhaps like you, have simply accepted consciousness as a "given" in human nature, and have, in truth, thought little about alternative scenarios. But some European developmentalists have given much thought and spent much time observing phenomena relating to consciousness, and their conclusions are broadly consistent with what I have suggested above.

Jean Piaget (1976), for example, proposed that consciousness is relatively late developing, and that it is preceded by behavior regulation that is automatic, rather than conscious. We, as adults, tend to think that conscious attention is most important when we are first learning a skill (downhill skiing, for instance) and that later, when we get better and better at the skill, it then becomes automatized. But according to Piaget, this course of development is reversed: we first learn sensory and motor adjustments, and it is only later (and quite imperfectly) that they can become the object of conscious awareness. He states, "Becoming conscious consists of a reconstruction on a higher level of something that is already organized, but differently, on a lower level" (1973, p. 256).

Expanding on this idea, Annette Karmiloff-Smith (1991, 1992), a one-time collaborator of Piaget's, has studied children's corrections of speech errors, and on the basis of these data, has proposed a three-stage process of development. In the first stage, knowledge is externally driven and procedural: we learn how to act in specific situations. Next, this level of knowledge is overlaid by knowledge that is cognitively accessible, that is, by symbolic knowledge that no longer requires the support of the environment for its processing. But while it is cognitively (or, in Karmiloff-Smith's account "computationally") accessible, such symbolic knowledge is not, at first, *consciously* accessible. The final stage is one at which symbolic knowledge is at least partly consciously accessible. Karmiloff-Smith's point is that consciousness is not always simply there, ever ready to address the world or the products of one's own cognition, but "gaining conscious access to represented knowledge is a constructive process which takes developmental time" (1986, p. 103).

The two related ideas of Piaget and Karmiloff-Smith are that consciousness is a construction, and that, as such, it is achieved only slowly across the first few years of human life. Neither of these authors, however, considered dreaming in this light. (Piaget [1962] did give an account of children's dreaming, but it consists, surprisingly, of much stale borrowing from Freud, buttressed with anecdotal dream data from his own children [see Foulkes, 1982b for a critique]). My data on children's dreams are, nonetheless, entirely consistent with Piaget's and Karmiloff-Smith's views of consciousness and its development.

It is a further virtue of the constructivist account of consciousness that it explains certain exotic forms of human consciousness, such as near-death experiences (Blackmore, 1988), for instance, in which the patient sees the doctor working on her as if from above the operating table. Such experiences totally elude the hypothesis that the contents of consciousness are inherent givens. This scene is not "given" by the patient's sense data; rather, it is the story most consistent with the scant information then available to her.

By far the best window we have for examining the development of consciousness is the laboratory dream report of the young child. In describing whether a dream has been experienced children are telling us whether they are able to simulate reality from information within the cognitive system. In telling us the events of a dream they are telling us how well developed that capacity is. There is quite simply no other laboratory operation for studying consciousness and its development that begins to match the directness and the richness of the lowly dream report. And from children's dream reporting in conditions of high cortical and cognitive arousal (that is, REM sleep) we learn that consciousness is a slowly developing process, and we are given some indication of just how late it is that such arousal *generally* is associated with conscious states. It is some time between when a child first becomes capable of having some REM dreaming and when the child almost invariably experiences such dreaming.

Next we learn that the whole *raison d'être* of consciousness is *organization, the integration of information*. In dreaming, the mind integrates currently active information, no matter how insusceptible to integration such information sometimes seems to be. Information is integrated both momentarily, as in particular dream imagery, and across time, as in dream stories. Dreams, children's earliest examples as well as our own, generally are coherent both momentarily and sequentially.

We also learn from dreams that narrative is the preferred form of the serial integration of consciousness, once serial conscious states themselves become possible. Whether "real" or not, conscious mental life presents itself to us as seamlessly interconnected events in narrative form. Although this narrative imperative is sufficiently strong to suggest that it is intrinsic to the human brain/mind, there is also evidence that it is shaped experientially. Through experience, we develop "scripts" (Mandler, 1984), or packages of expectations about what typically happens in certain culturally defined situations. When we go to the movies, for instance, we may expect to stand in line, to buy tickets, to enter the theater, to buy refreshments, to find a seat, to see previews of coming attractions, to see the movie, and to exit the theater. Much of the everyday realism of representatively sampled REM dreams comes from their adherence to these scripts of everyday life.

In addition, dreams indicate that, as Piaget and Inhelder's (1969, 1971) research also showed, the first mental imagery seems to be static and rather unversatile, and that "Kinetic and transformational images are possible only after [ages] seven or eight" (1969, p. 77). The biggest surprise of all, of course, is the lateness of the appearance of a simulated active self-representation.

Consciousness and the Self

Childhood dreaming's most significant revelation is that of the intimate relationship between consciousness and the development of *self-identity*. After its halting initial efforts, children's consciousness is organized narratively across time through the medium of a continuing sense of self. By age 8 or so this seems to be a frequent, if not invariant, feature of children's dreams.

In the realm of wakefulness, this relatively late appearance of conscious self-identity across time suggests a stark phenomenological difference between the experience of young children (and animals) and our own. But could young children and other animals behave as sensibly and sensitively as they sometimes do without our sense of conscious self-continuity? I believe that they can do just that.

I will cite, not anthropomorphically as most often is the case with animal anecdotes, but contra-anthropomorphically, my experiences with a pet, my frequent daytime companion of the past several years, a dog named "Cracker." In my observation, Cracker is, behaviorally, not one dog but many. In the early morning, when she comes in to waken me, Cracker is extraordinarily gentle and loving. Minutes later, when we emerge outdoors for the day's first walk, she is all business, exploring nature and chasing squirrels with apparently total obliviousness toward my presence. When she reluctantly returns home, she is, evidently buoyed by the experience of her walk, aggressively naughty, barking and jumping up, so as to interfere with my coffee-drinking and newspaper-reading. Quickly, however, she will settle in place, draped over the sofa, looking out the window, half asleep, once again placid and gentle. The remarkable thing about these different behavioral selves is that they seem to have little contact with one another. While she is aggressive, she may "accidentally" bite me, and I get mad and scold her. But a few minutes later she is being gentle with me again as if nothing had happened to alter our relationship. As often has been noted, one of the nice things about dogs is that, unlike adults, they don't harbor grudges and they quickly seem to forget life's little unpleasantnesses.

The story here probably is that they *can't* harbor grudges and let moods get them down, because they don't have the conscious sense of self that would let them build bridges between sequential situations in their experience. At Moment 2, there is, in an important sense, a different dog than there was at Moment 1. The Moment-2 dog is defined not by any conscious continuity of identity with the Moment-1 dog, but by the behavioral traits generally associated in the past with Situation 2.

It may not be so different with very young children. The child, at her Moment 2, often fails to see why the parent isn't acting as he or she should in such a moment, because her expectations, unmediated by conscious self-continuity, are keyed to past situations of the Moment-2 type, while the parent's expectations are keyed to how the child may have acted at Moment 1. Thus Mommy, still infuriated by the child's tantrum at the picnic table, now refuses to push the child's swing; the child, however, is now in a new but familiar situation, with no conscious links in self-identity back to what has happened immediately prior to that situation. She can't understand why Mommy won't push the swing.

One of the offshoots of the recent appearance/fabrication of so many multiple-personality phenomena (Spanos, 1996) in courtrooms and tabloid television has been a reexamination of the development of self-identity in early childhood. Perhaps young children, it has been suggested, are multiple personalities—in the less florid sense exhibited by the dog Cracker. Perhaps it is only slowly that the kind of self-identity evolves which begins to integrate the child's different behavioral selves exhibited in her various repetitive life situations. The evidence of the late appearance of self-identity in children's dreaming consciousness suggests that the above waking scenario is a plausible one, that conscious self-identity is how the early multiplicity of behaving selves is integrated developmentally, and that the study of children's dreams might be used to index the course of this development.

In this light, it is interesting to consider children who never seem to develop much of a conscious sense of self or the ability to reflect upon either the world or themselves: autistic children. In her book on autism, Uta Frith (1989) notes that the typical intellectual profile of the autistic child (of whom 75% are mentally retarded) is one of *relative* excellence on Wechsler Block Design and relative weakness in Verbal Comprehension. She attributes the higher quality of Block Design performance to its relative independence from "high-level central thought processes" (p. 102).

But the data from children's dreaming suggest, to the contrary, that a high Block Design score reveals the capacity for having the most conspicuous high-level thought process of them all—consciousness. Given that autistic children exhibit absent or defective self-awareness, how can we understand their relatively high Block Design scores? First, we need to understand that, even though there often seem to be earlier signs, autism first reveals itself as a clinical syndrome between ages 3 and 5. There are no subhuman forms of autism. Autism therefore must involve the misdevelopment of something distinctively human, appearing generally between the ages 3 and 5. That something is consciousness: the ability not just to see and hear and feel but the simultaneous awareness that you are doing these things.

We know very little, obviously, about the related cognitive developments on which consciousness builds. In its application to dreaming, Block Design seems to measure something that contributes to the appearance and subsequent development of consciousness. Without a certain level of Block Design performance, whatever one's age, dreaming either seems not to happen at all or not to happen very reliably. But Block Design is not the only kind of intellectual skill that has been correlated with dreaming in early childhood, and certain forms of dream expression, narration, for instance, seem to depend as much on verbal as on visual or spatial skills.

For most children, mental skills of different sorts develop more or less together and at a standard rate. Suppose, however, that autistic children have the capacity for conscious representation without having, either absolutely or relative to their other skills, the tools to organize and utilize conscious representations. This surely would be a hollow kind of consciousness, and, compared to simple mental retardation, a bewildering and disorienting state of affairs, one which, once set in motion, might later prove to be irreversible. Could this be the defining cognitive defect of autism? It has often been thought that autistic persons experience life incoherently, as disconnected happenings. There is developing awareness, but this awareness lacks coherence.

Which raises an interesting question: do autistic children or adults dream? And if so, how? I pretend to no knowledge here.

But a computer data search (in 1996) of recent scientific literature has produced no reports of autistic dreaming, and revealed remarkably little interest in the possibility. Frith (1989, p. 31) uses the awareness of dreaming (in discussing the historically famous case of Kasper Hauser) as a contraindication of autism. It is possible that the sleep laboratory could provide some information on the inner mental status of autistic children. Difficult as it is to imagine how one might proceed, it certainly still might be worth some effort thinking through the possibilities.

In one of the standardized tests of self-identity (Guardo & Bohan, 1971) that we used with the cross-sectional sample, each child was asked whether he/she was the same person now as when a baby. By conventional scoring criteria, children could claim that they were the same, and receive a score indicating a mature knowledge of self. But I look at the current data on the development of conscious cognition (including dreaming), and I wonder. Where there is not yet the capacity for any genuine kind of human consciousness, much less conscious self-representation, where there is not yet an autobiographical memory built around conscious episodic reflection, is there any meaningful sense in which an infantile self exists, much less one which has temporal continuity to later years? From the parents' perspective, it may seem like the same person, but what does it mean to the creature originally unconscious of its own potential for personhood and only now beginning to realize that potential?

It is difficult for me not to think that there's a far more interesting story about development in the first 5 or 7 years of human life than one finds in most psychology textbooks, with their detailed accounts of infantile precocities and the implication that such early skills lie along a path of continuous human intellectual advancement. There can be little doubt but that developmentalists have uncovered heretofore unappreciated infantile skills, ones that make eminent sense from an adaptive point of view. But it is doubtful that these skills are integral to the development of what makes us distinctively human—reflective consciousness and personhood.

Infants are not little versions of ourselves, and what they can do does not necessarily mark the start of some steady developmental continuum leading to ourselves. In addition to focusing attention on *what* infants and young children can do or say, we need to attend to *how* they do what they do. The evidence of this book suggests that their approach to the world and the developing operations of their own minds is fundamentally different from our own, and that the difference is one of automatic versus conscious mediation.

The 5 to 7 shift in waking cognitive maturation was described and labeled in a paper published by Sheldon White in 1965. In American developmental psychology's more recent period of establishing precocious cognitive competencies in infancy and the preschool years, the apparent qualitative shift in cognitive competencies between ages 5 and 7 was put on the back burner as an issue for either research or theory.

More recently, however, thanks to the MacArthur Foundation Research Network on Early Childhood Transitions, attention has returned to the 5 to 7 shift, as evidenced by a volume on that phenomenon edited by Sameroff and Haith (1996). Dreaming does not, of course, figure in this reassessment. Nor do the authors of the various chapters (with one exception, the Genevan psychologist Mounoud [1996]), consider that consciousness *per se* might underlie the shift. But the findings they report—new and different ways of accessing memories, the development of the ability to reflect on one's own memories, the development of episodic contextualization of memories, the development of the ability to observe and to criticize oneself—do lend themselves to the interpretation of newly conscious mediation of self-world interaction.

Now, it should be understood that I am not espousing the view that consciousness suddenly appears one day and immediately transforms or reorganizes all prior cognitive skills. Such a view would clearly not be consistent with the complex nature of the evidence on waking cognitive shifts around ages 5 to 7. Nor, of course, would it be consistent with the dream evidence itself on which my view is based. That evidence suggests no miraculous, instantaneous, general shifts in the child's cognition, but rather a gradual and protracted set of developing competencies that eventually issue into something like the kind of conscious cognition with which we adults are familiar.

Consciousness is not a luxury afforded full-blown to creatures born as immature as we are and facing as much to learn as we do. Elementary habits and skills of adaptation first are learned without it. Consciousness emerges slowly, once such learning is well under way, and its eventual scope is not even approached until the early grade-school years. With the emergence of active self-representation, of autobiographical memory, and of a sensed self that lends continuity to experience, the human person emerges. Whatever this person's behavioral continuities with the past, experientially there is discontinuity. No, I am not the same person now as when I was a baby, because then I was no person at all.

Dream data have brought us this far in understanding human development, and they remain our best source of information on the development of an inner (meaning, a conscious) mental life. Freud (1900) thought that *"The interpretation of dreams is the royal road to a knowledge of the unconscious activities of the mind* (1955 edition, p. 608)." But he achieved no reliable knowledge through his kind of dream interpretation. I now suggest an alternative formulation, "The study of dreaming is the royal road to understanding the unfolding of consciousness and personhood in early childhood." I hope that one hundred years from now, this formulation will be somewhat more successful than Freud's has proved to be after a century, in generating reliable knowledge about our specifically human development as consciously aware persons.

Appendix
Two Children's Dream Reports over Time
~

Here are the REM dream reports of Dean and his sister Emily, who served, respectively, in the younger and older longitudinal study groups. The reports have been edited for clarity of reading, hence they are not verbatim transcriptions of the original taped interviews.

The numbering of a report indicates, in turn, the night of the study year on which it was collected, and the awakening time (of 3) on that night. Thus Dean's report 1-2 from Year 1 came from the second awakening on the first study night of that year. Awakening 1 was scheduled to occur somewhere between 11 P.M. and 1 A.M., awakening 2 was scheduled to occur at approximately 3 A.M., and awakening 3 was scheduled to occur somewhere between 4 and 6 A.M.

Dean's REM Dreams

Year 1
Age at year onset: 4 years, 8 months
REM recall rate: dreams reported on 2 of 15 REM awakenings (13%)

1-2   I was asleep and in the bathtub.

7-3   I was sleeping at a co-co stand, where you get Coke from.

Year 3

Age at year onset: 6 years, 8 months

REM recall rate: dreams reported on 5 of 15 REM awakenings (33%)

1-1 A cabin at Barbara Lake. It was little, and I looked in it. Freddie [friend and fellow participant in the study] and I were playing around, with a few toys and things.

2-1 Some guy swimming, and baseball at high school.

2-3 Cows on the ranch, just mooing, just running around. I could see the ranch house.

8-1 A running race, John and I, on the playground. Johnny won.

8-3 I was building a car bridge with Lego blocks in my room at home. My bed was in a different place. I drove cars on the bridges.

Year 5

Age at year onset: 8 years, 8 months

REM recall rate: dreams reported on 11 of 15 REM awakenings (73%)

1-1 We were supposed to come here and sleep. Only, when we came here, we had a party and Freddie [same name, but different friend than above] got a bike. Freddie, and John, and Kate, and Freddie [the first one] were there. You were in your office, putting on the wires. They had a big cake, and everybody was giving out gifts. I got a weight-lift.

1-3 Another boy, a made-up one, and I were on a mountain, hiking.

2-1 I went skiing at a place, and I broke my leg. I went again, and nothing happened. So I kept going, and then I broke it again, so I finally quit, and I started to take up another sport, swimming. There were other skiers and swimmers, all kinds of people. The pool was indoors. I was sad when I broke my leg, and glad to get the cast off my leg. Dr. V. [a local surgeon] took it off.

2-3 We were tree planters, my friends and I, about 5 boys, and we went up to this place and planted a tree. And the next day we came back, and the tree was already grown. So we planted more, and they all grew. We had tree seeds, and we planted them. And there was a forest fire, and they wouldn't burn down. So we made forests out of them. We walked all around the forest. And then some men were chopping them down for firewood, and when they chopped them down, the fire wouldn't work. So they told it to the State Police, and the Mayor said that they planted trees, and they won't burn. I was excited because those trees wouldn't burn, and they grew every day.

3-2 One day, my mom, she got my sister some skis—she got all three sisters some skis—and I didn't get any skis. It took too long, and they didn't have any small enough sizes. And she got a letter, that we could go skiing up at Steamboat Springs, and I couldn't go, because I didn't have any skis. And so I didn't go, but when they got back, they had gotten me some skis. Then I got to go skiing up at Happy Jack [a closer, and less grand, ski area] with them.

4-3 There was this boy in Africa, and he had a parrot, a mouse, and a lion. And he told the mouse to do something—I don't know what—and the mouse came back, and he didn't do it. And then the mouse went back and he died. And all the boy had was this parrot and this lion.

He told them to stay there, and he was going to go out and catch an elephant, because he had to pull logs to stop the water from coming in. And he set up a pit, and the elephant came, and fell in the pit. But the pit was too little and the elephant got out. And so he tried a sleeping pill, and he stuck it in some weeds, and the elephant came along and ate it, and he fell asleep. And the boy took him, and (indistinct) him, and got the whatever-you-call-it fixed, and it all went pretty good.

5-1   There was this hippo, and he got out of the zoo. And he got into this big van, with a guy driving it, and went to a far country in Africa, and was living there. And people—Indians, about five of them—were trying to hunt him and stuff. I was excited when they were trying to hunt them; I wanted him not to get caught. So then he went back to the zoo, and everything was peaceful again.

6-2   My family—my sisters and my mom—and I were going on a trip skiing. We were flying there. I could see the airplane, and the people and things at an airport. And when I turned around, I took the wrong plane, and I went to the Olympics instead. I got worried when I went to the Olympics, because I missed the plane. I could see the people at the Olympics, they had a torch, and people skiing and stuff.

7-3   I was dreaming about when I got a puppy. It's not really my puppy. It was a small dog, and he was brown. And so we went to this place, and they asked me if I wanted to name it something else, and I didn't. So we took it home, and I gave it a bath. I was happy when I was giving him a bath.

8-3 We were going to get a new dog. I saw a dog in the pet store, so I went in to the store man, I was asking the clerk for a dog, and he said I could have it. There was a whole bunch of animals there, monkeys and birds and gerbils. And then I went home, and asked my mom if I could buy it. She said I could, and I was just getting the dog in the pet shop [when awakened]. I was happy when I got the dog. He was a small one.

9-2 I found some balloons in a park, and I untied them from a tree. I wanted to get one balloon, but I untied the thing that was tied to the tree. And as I was hanging on to them, I floated into the air. I was in the sky. And I couldn't get them down, and I was scared when I couldn't get down from the balloons.

Emily's REM Dreams

Year 1

Age at year onset: 10 years, 5 months

REM recall rate: dreams reported on 14 of 15 REM awakenings (93%)

1-2 I dreamed about the sleep-lab's nursery school, and the little nursery-school kids. There were only three kids there. I recognized Dean, he's my little brother. It looked like it was happening in a gym or somewhere. And then the kids were leaving, and going up the stairs. And the nursery-school teacher said good-bye.

1-3 There were some ladies walking down the hall, talking to each other. Two people were walking together, and one person was walking alone. It looked like it was in a school.

2-1 I was just listening to a song.

2-3 There was a little boy and two girls, and they lived in our house. The little boy wanted to play, so he came out into the kitchen, and asked the mother if he could play with his blocks in his room. So he went out and played, and the two girls stayed in the kitchen, sitting at the table, eating. They were looking at the mail. The little boy was about five years old, and the girls were about eleven.

3-2 I was playing with the two twins that live next door to me and my sister. We were playing something with a rope, it might have been jump-rope, on the driveway of our house. We were having fun playing.

4-1 There was a lady and she was on the TV show *Gilligan's Island,* and in a Comet [cleanser] Josephine commercial too. She didn't do anything on the show, but in the commercial she was crying about her house, because it was so old and torn up. The lady is really on *Gilligan's Island,* but in the dream she was doing a Comet commercial with the plumber, Josephine.

4-3 Costumes there at a birthday party, and you go and dress up like an animal. There were these two guys, and they were ice-skating on a rink, dressed up like bears. Some other guys were making a cake, and some guys were playing with trains, and I was there, but I don't remember what I was wearing. My next-door neighbor girlfriend was playing with me. It was up in the mountains somewhere.

5-1 A rug, on the floor. Kids were in a house, I don't know which one. It was near Christmas, like it is now, and someone said that next year at Halloween we'd have to get another costume for Halloween before Christmas came. And then he said, "Well, it's after Halloween now."

6-2 Bears and snakes. The bears were outside someplace in the mountains, on the left side, growling. The snakes were on the right side, moving around. I wasn't in it, and had no feelings.

7-2 Some doctors, about six, looking down the hall of some hospital.

7-3 I was in school, and the teacher was up at the board, talking and writing on the blackboard, and showing us something. We have some SRA [Science Research Associates] things in school, and she was telling us we had to hand in one SRA thing, talking about how we'd have to do it. It was my real teacher, and my real school. I was doing a "powerbuilder" exercise in SRA.

8-1 A guy was at a microphone, and I don't know what caused it, but he moved, and the microphone fell down, fell off. It was on a stage someplace.

8-3 It was a nice night before Easter, and we had company over at our house. And nobody would get into bed. There was a big fight, and everybody was crying. There were two boys in the bedroom, and they were throwing an inflatable bunny back and forth. Another girl was in the living room, crying. And a girl popped another girl's balloon, and then she got mad at her, and they started having a fight. The people were neighbors that live next door to me on both sides, and some people we know that live downtown, and the rest of my family, except my parents. They had already gone to bed. But it didn't look the same, our living room was in the wrong place. I was kind of mad, nobody would go to bed, and I was trying to get them to.

9-2 A crate of oranges, with some great big ones and some real little ones. A woman, I don't know who it was, was picking up a big orange, and there was some brown paper stuck in between the little oranges. I was there, watching him [sic] take the oranges out. It was indoors somewhere.

Year 3

Age at year onset: 12 years, 5 months

REM recall rate: dreams reported on 12 of 14 REM awakenings (86%)

1-2 I was in a room, with a table and some chairs, and another person, I think it was a girl about my age. She was telling me a joke, and asked me to measure a foot. So I put down the length of my foot. She said it was wrong because a foot had to be 12 inches long. She was standing up, and telling me what I was supposed to do, and I was writing down what I thought was the answer to the thing.

2-1 There were these four girls, sitting around a table in a great big room, and one had some homemade butter. One person put it on bread, another put it on oysters or something like that. They were all telling the girl how good the butter was.

2-3 My sister was playing with those little tiny dolls, and she had her big dollhouse with all this little furniture. I was holding my hamster and a little tiny dog—it was alive—and I went to put it to bed in that dollhouse, but I couldn't, because my sisters were playing with it. We have a dog, but not that little—it was real tiny. My real dog was in the dream too. It happened in a living room, but it wasn't ours. I was moving around there, and my sisters were moving around the dollhouse, using their hands to move the dolls.

3-2   There was this line of bookshelves, and a boy was putting the books in them. He was doing it just any old way, not doing it right. He was sitting on his knees, handling the books. It took place in a room in some house.

4-1   I dreamed about a girl I have band class with. She was all dressed up, and had a lunch ticket in her hand. She was standing on the sidewalk on a sunny day. There were trees in the background, but I didn't know where it was. She was telling me how much she hated the guy who used to go to her school. I asked her, "What is that guy's last name?" and she told me. It's not some name I really know.

4-3   I was in a car with two friends of mine, and another girl, and her mother, who was French, was driving us home. She had a French accent and was talking to us. And there was something in the street that was mine, and I told them that that was my choker out there in the street. And so we stopped, and one friend got out to get it. And this other guy, her father, he was in the car too, he just drove off and left her there, standing out in the middle of the street. And we were all just looking at each other in the car, wondering. At the end of the dream I was kind of excited, because he left her out there in the street all alone, and kind of angry toward him.

5-1 A bunch of ladies were in a band, and they all wore long dresses, instead of uniforms, and they marched in the street, playing songs and stuff. It was kind of fast music, like a regular band would play. I remember watching the trombone being played. I was kind of excited by the band going by with just the women in it, playing fast music.

6-2 I was sitting in a bed, and my brother Dean [co-participant on this laboratory night] asked me to read something to him on the page of a book. I didn't have my glasses on, and I said, "I can't read it; it's too far away." Then I got up out of bed. It was in the bedroom of some house. Dean was just sitting in the bed, reading the book, just looking at the pictures. I wasn't too interested in reading to him.

7-2 I was on the set of the television show *Bewitched.* They were having this party there. The Samantha character was there. My little cousin, *her* cousin Serena, was there too—Elizabeth Montgomery plays both characters. There were other girls at the party, I don't know who though, standing around talking like in a theater party. I was talking, but not saying very much, because Samantha was talking to me most of the time. She said that I was supposed to go have some snacks or something like that. Then, when her cousin came, she said "Serena," and that's when I woke up.

7-3 I was talking to my father in our kitchen. He said that if you swallow something, then you can't get it back out. Then he said something like, anyone who was determined could swallow anything, or something like that. And I said, yes, if you tie a piece of string to it, you can get it back out. Because there is this experiment in my last year's science book where a guy put food in his mouth, and waited until it went through his digestive system, and then he'd pull it back out. To illustrate, I had a piece of hair or something that I swallowed, and then I just took it back out. My mother came in, about in the middle, and was talking about some science classes, but I wasn't listening to her.

8-1   I was skiing at Medicine Bow [local ski area] with my dad. I saw a bunch of trees, then a great big, long, tall one, then it was a T-bar tow, and a bunch of people were on the tow. The tows were closer together, like one right after another, than they really are. I just remember us going up the tow. There was a great big line or something, and my dad didn't want me to ski there. I told him he should go to Jackson [400 miles away] or something; I was not joking, but serious.

8-3   I was walking in the street with a girlfriend, who was on a bike. I was looking at the flowers in these people's yards, and I said, "Oh, look at the flowers." Then I drove, I mean I walked, over to this big pile of dirt in Washington Park. And my friend was going to show me something, but then I woke up. Before we came over to her house, there was this one boy with a great big duffle bag, and he was sitting on it, looking around the corner.

Year 5

Age at year onset: 14 years, 5 months

REM recall rate: dreams reported on 13 of 15 REM awakenings (87%)

1-1 I was getting ready to take a gymnastics lesson. It was in the middle of the country somewhere, and there was a mat on the ground. Everybody that was going to take the lesson was standing around on the mat; there were about eight or ten of us, some were older women and some were about my own age. There was a teacher, but she wasn't doing anything yet. I was just standing there, and I think I was talking. I was kind of worried or excited, because I was waiting for it to start, and I was worried that it wasn't going to start on time.

1-2 Somebody was throwing candy at a parade, but there weren't any floats or anything. They were just throwing them into the street; I didn't know where it was coming from, really. And I went out and got it. It was just me, I guess, I was alone.

1-3 I was dishing some water out of the well with a ladle. I was going to give it to my friend, only she didn't want it. I don't know where it was, it just didn't have a setting. There was one more person in it, a man standing around the well.

2-1 I had some sort of disease or something on my tonsils. I didn't know what it was. I was looking at them in the mirror, and I didn't see anything at all. I was alone, in some house somewhere, or something. I guess I was kind of worried about the disease.

2-3 I was playing some kind of game. We had to hide behind somebody's room, to hide something behind somebody's room, where somebody couldn't find it. I think it was at our house, only the rooms were changed around a little different. And after that was over, we all rode down the hill by our house on our ten-speed bicycles, me and my younger sister.

3-2 I was at school, and I was cleaning out my locker. I had to bring my mom's gloves home, because I'd taken them to school, and forgotten to bring them home. I had just remembered that I had to bring them home, so I was trying to find them. And I did, and took them out, and left.

4-1 I had to do a dance in front of a whole bunch of people. I had different socks, and I had great big holes in the bottom of my socks, and I didn't know it. It was on some stage, with a whole bunch of adults in the show watching. I think it was before an audience too, but I couldn't see the audience. I looked and saw my socks, and felt embarrassed.

4-3 I had this green-tipped pen, and it was one of the kind that you can switch the needles on, with all these different colors. I was trying to figure out how to do it, and I didn't know how. A friend was with me, she was just looking at the pen, while I was working at it. I couldn't tell where we were. My friend asked me what it was, and I told her it was a pen. And she said, "That doesn't make any sense," because she didn't think it looked like a pen at all. It was like a great big piece of pipe, about eight inches long. I was trying to put one of the pen things out, so I could write with it, because they were all inside. I wasn't finished with it. I was still working; I think I knew how to do it.

6-2 I was with a bunch of girls on a bus that was coming back from the state basketball tournament, talking about people that lost money at the tournament. I just said, somebody lost some money, but I can't remember who. And somebody said somebody else did too.

7-2   My mom was at a sewing-club meeting in the living room at our house, and she was getting everybody some coffee. It was a bunch of her friends, and she was walking around the room, pouring, and they were drinking their coffee and talking. I wasn't in the dream.

7-3   I was dragging around a great big bow, made of ribbon, pulling it around on the floor. It was about five feet long, and the ribbon was a half an inch wide. I think it was indoors, but I don't know where. This was just the whole dream.

8-3   I was up in the mountains somewhere. And there was a town in the country, and a really fat lady who worked in a store there. She had glasses, and didn't remind me of anybody I know. I could see the counter, it was wood, and there was a cash register on it. It was an old-fashioned store. And she had a bunch of pet dogs and a bunch of pet mice that she let run all over the neighborhood. Then she'd call them, and they'd all come back to her. I went around and petted all the dogs. She called them something, and they just ran up and gathered around her. I think there were three big dogs, and the rest were little. They were all the same kind, only different colors. The mice were just all the same.

9-2   An Indian, he had on an Indian suit, walking. I couldn't see where.

References

Antrobus, J. S. (1983). REM and NREM sleep reports: Comparison of word frequencies by cognitive classes. *Psychophysiology, 20,* 562–568.

Arkin, A. M. (1981). *Sleep-talking: Psychology and psychophysiology.* Hillsdale NJ: Lawrence Erlbaum Associates.

Arkin, A. M., Antrobus, J. S., and Ellman, S. J. (Eds.) (1978). *The mind in sleep: Psychology and psychophysiology.* Hillsdale NJ: Lawrence Erlbaum Associates.

Aserinsky, E. and Kleitman, N. (1953). Regularly occurring periods of eye motility, and concomitant phenomena, during sleep. *Science, 118,* 273–274.

Blackmore, S. (1988). A theory of lucid dreams and OBEs. In J. Gackenbach and S. LaBerge (Eds.), *Conscious mind, sleeping brain: Perspectives on lucid dreaming* (pp. 373–387). New York: Plenum Press.

Butler, S. F. and Watson, R. (1985). Individual differences in memory for dreams: The role of cognitive skills. *Perceptual and Motor Skills, 61,* 823–828.

Cavallero, C. and Cicogna, P. (1993). Memory and dreaming. In C. Cavallero and D. Foulkes (Eds.), *Dreaming as cognition* (pp. 38–57). London: Harvester Wheatsheaf.

Damon, W. and Hart, D. (1988). *Self-understanding in childhood and adolescence.* Cambridge UK: Cambridge University Press.

DeMartino, M. F. (1955). A review of the literature on children's dreams. *Psychiatric Quarterly Supplement, 29,* Part 1, 90–101.

Dement, W. and Kleitman, N. (1957). The relation of eye movements during sleep to dream activity: An objective method for the study of dreaming. *Journal of Experimental Psychology, 53,* 339–346.

Domhoff, B. (1969). Home dreams versus laboratory dreams: Home dreams are better. In M. Kramer (Ed.), *Dream psychology and the new biology of dreaming* (pp. 199–217). Springfield IL: Charles C Thomas.

Domhoff, G. W. (1996). *Finding meaning in dreams: A quantitative approach.* New York: Plenum Press.

Dorus, E., Dorus, W., and Rechtschaffen A. (1971). The incidence of novelty in dreams. *Archives of General Psychiatry, 25,* 364–368.

Feinberg, I. (1969). Effects of age on human sleep patterns. In A. Kales (Ed.), *Sleep: Physiology and pathology* (pp. 39–52). Philadelphia: J. B. Lippincott.

Flavell, J. H. (1963). *The developmental psychology of Jean Piaget.* Princeton NJ: D. Van Nostrand.

Foulkes, D. (1962). Dream reports from different stages of sleep. *Journal of Abnormal and Social Psychology, 65,* 14–25.

Foulkes, D. (1966). *The psychology of sleep.* New York: Charles Scribner's Sons.

Foulkes, D. (1967). Dreams of the male child: Four case studies. *Journal of Child Psychology and Psychiatry, 8,* 81–98.

Foulkes, D. (1978). *A grammar of dreams.* New York: Basic Books.

Foulkes, D. (1979). Home and laboratory dreams: Four empirical studies and a conceptual reevaluation. *Sleep, 2,* 233–251.

Foulkes, D. (1982a). *Children's dreams: Longitudinal studies.* New York: Wiley-Interscience.

Foulkes, D. (1982b). REM-dream perspectives on the development of affect and cognition. *Psychiatric Journal of the University of Ottawa, 7,* 48–55.

Foulkes, D. (1983). Cognitive processes during sleep: Evolutionary aspects. In A. Mayes (Ed.), *Sleep mechanisms and functions in humans and animals: An evolutionary perspective* (pp. 313–337). Wokington UK: Van Nostrand Reinhold.

Foulkes, D. (1985). *Dreaming: A cognitive-psychological analysis.* Hillsdale NJ: Lawrence Erlbaum Associates.

Foulkes, D. (1996a). Dream research: 1953–1993. *Sleep, 19,* 609–624.

Foulkes, D. (1996b). Misrepresentation of sleep-laboratory dream research with children. *Perceptual and Motor Skills, 83,* 205–206.

Foulkes, D. and Bradley, L. (1989). Phasic activity and dream recall in 5- to 8-yr.-olds. *Perceptual and Motor Skills, 69,* 290.

Foulkes, D. and Fleisher, S. (1975). Mental activity in relaxed wakefulness. *Journal of Abnormal Psychology, 84,* 66–75.

Foulkes, D. and Hollifield, M. (1989). Responses to picture-plane and depth mental-rotation stimuli in children and adults. *Bulletin of the Psychonomic Society, 27,* 327–330.

Foulkes, D., Hollifield, M., Bradley, L., Terry, R, and Sullivan, B. (1991). Waking self-understanding, REM-dream self representation, and cognitive ability variables at ages 5–8. *Dreaming, 1,* 41–51.

Foulkes, D., Hollifield, M., Sullivan, B., Bradley, L., and Terry, R. (1990). REM dreaming and cognitive skills at ages 5–8: A cross-sectional study. *International Journal of Behavioral Development, 13,* 447–465.

Foulkes, D., Larson, J. D., Swanson, E. M., and Rardin, M. W. (1969). Two studies of childhood dreaming. *American Journal of Orthopsychiatry, 39,* 627–643.

Foulkes, D., Pivik, T., Steadman, H. E., Spear, P. S., and Symonds, J. D. (1967). Dreams of the male child: An EEG study. *Journal of Abnormal Psychology, 72,* 457–467.

Foulkes, D. and Schmidt, M. (1983). Temporal sequence and unit composition in dream reports from different stages of sleep. *Sleep, 6,* 265–280.

Foulkes, D. and Scott, E. (1973). An above-zero waking baseline for the incidence of momentarily hallucinatory mentation. *Sleep Research, 2,* 108.

Foulkes, D. and Shepherd, J. (1971). *Manual for a scoring system for children's dreams.* Laramie WY: authors.

Foulkes, D., Sullivan, B., Hollifield, M., and Bradley, L. (1989). Mental rotation, age, and conservation. *Journal of Genetic Psychology, 150,* 449–451.

Foulkes, D., Sullivan, B., Kerr, N. H., and Brown, L. (1988). Appropriateness of dream feelings to dreamed situations. *Cognition and Emotion, 2,* 29–39.

Foulkes, D. and Vogel. G. (1965). Mental activity at sleep onset. *Journal of Abnormal Psychology, 70,* 231–243.

Frith, U. (1989). *Autism: Explaining the enigma.* Oxford: Basil Blackwell.

Freud, S. (1899). Screen memories (trans. by J. Strachey). In P. Rieff (Ed.), *Freud: Early psychoanalytic writings* (pp. 229–250). New York: Collier Books, 1963.

Freud, S. (1900). *The interpretation of dreams* (trans. by J. Strachey). New York: Basic Books, 1955.

Gardiner, M. (Ed.) (1971). *The wolf-man.* New York: Basic Books.

Garfield, P. (1984). *Your child's dreams.* New York: Ballantine.

Gennaro, R. J. (1996). *Consciousness and self-consciousness.* Philadelphia: John Benjamins.

Gruber, H. E. and Vonèche, J. J. (Eds.) (1977). *The essential Piaget.* New York: Basic Books.

Guardo, C. J. and Bohan, J. B. (1971). Development of a sense of self-identity in children. *Child Development, 42,* 1909–1921.

Hacking, I. (1995). *Rewriting the soul: Multiple personality and the sciences of memory.* Princeton NJ: Princeton University Press.

Hall, C. S. and Van de Castle, R. L. (1966). *The content analysis of dreams.* New York: Appleton-Century-Crofts.

Hobson, J. A. (1988). *The dreaming brain.* New York: Basic Books.

Hobson, J. A. and McCarley, R. W. (1977). The brain as a dream state generator: An activation-synthesis hypothesis of the dream process. *American Journal of Psychiatry, 134,* 1335–1348.

Humphrey, G. (1951). *Thinking: An introduction to its experimental psychology.* New York: John Wiley & Sons.

Hunt, H. T. (1989). *The multiplicity of dreams: Memory, imagination, and consciousness.* New Haven CT: Yale University Press.

Jacobson, A., Kales, A., Lehmann, D., and Zweizig, J. R. (1965). Somnambulism: All-night electroencephalographic studies. *Science, 148,* 975–977.

James, W. (1890). *The principles of psychology* (2 vols.). New York: Holt.

Jastrow, J. (1900). *Fact and fable in psychology.* New York: Houghton Mifflin.

Jung, C. J. (1960). On the nature of dreams. In *Dreams* (trans. by R. F. C. Hull; pp. 67–83). Princeton NJ: Princeton University Press, 1974.

Jung, C. J. (1965). *Memories, dreams, and reflections* (trans. by R. Winston and C. Winston). New York: Vintage Books.

Kagan, J. and Moss, H. A. (1962). *Birth to maturity: A study in psychological development.* New York: John Wiley & Sons.

Kahn, R. L. and Cannell, C. F. (1957). *The dynamics of interviewing.* New York: John Wiley & Sons.

Kales, J. D., Jacobson, A., and Kales, A. (1969). Sleep disorders in children. *Progress in Clinical Psychology, 8,* 63–73.

Kales, J. D., Kales, A., Jacobson, A., Po, J., and Green, J. (1968). Baseline sleep and recall studies in children. *Psychophysiology, 4,* 391.

Karmiloff-Smith, A. (1986). From meta-processes to conscious access: Evidence from children's metalinguistic and repair data. *Cognition, 23,* 95–147.

Karmiloff-Smith, A. (1991). Beyond modularity: Innate constraints and developmental change. In S. Carey and R. Gelman (Eds.), *The epigenesis of mind: Essays on biology and cognition* (pp. 171–197). Hillsdale NJ: Lawrence Erlbaum Associates.

Karmiloff-Smith, A. (1992). *Beyond modularity: A developmental perspective on cognitive science.* Cambridge MA: MIT Press.

Kerr, N. H. (1993). Mental imagery, dreams, and perception. In C. Cavallero and D. Foulkes (Eds.), *Dreaming as cognition* (pp. 18–37). London: Harvester Wheatsheaf.

Kerr, N. H., Foulkes, D., and Schmidt, M. (1982). The structure of laboratory dream reports in blind and sighted subjects. *The Journal of Nervous and Mental Disease, 170,* 286–294.

Kohler, W. C., Coddington, R. D., and Agnew, H. W. (1968). Sleep patterns in 2-year-old children. *Journal of Pediatrics, 72,* 228–233.

Kramer, M. (1994). Introduction. *Dreaming, 4,* 43–46.

Kushida, C. A., Bergmann, B. M., and Rechtschaffen, A. (1989). Sleep deprivation in the rat: IV. Paradoxical sleep deprivation. *Sleep, 12,* 22–30.

Laurendeau, M. and Pinard, A. (1962). *Causal thinking in the child.* New York: International Universities Press.

Macnish, R. (1834). *The philosophy of sleep.* New York: D. Appleton.

Mandler, J. M. (1983). Representation. In J. H. Flavell and E. M. Markman (Eds.), *Handbook of child psychology: Vol. 3. Cognitive development* (pp. 420–494). New York: John Wiley & Sons.

Mandler, J. M. (1984). *Stories, scripts, and scenes: Aspects of schema theory.* Hillsdale NJ: Lawrence Erlbaum Associates.

Merton, R. K. (1957). *Social theory and social structure* (rev. ed.). Glencoe IL: The Free Press.

Moffitt, A., Kramer, M., and Hoffman, R. (Eds.) (1993). *The functions of dreaming.* Albany NY: SUNY Press.

Montangero, J., Pasche, P., and Willequet, P. (1996). Remembering and communicating the dream experience: What does a complementary morning report add to the night report? *Dreaming, 6,* 131–145.

Moscovitch, M. (Ed.) (1984). *Infant memory: Its relation to normal and pathological memory in humans and other animals.* New York: Plenum Press.

Mounoud, P. (1996). A recursive transformation of central cognitive mechanisms: The shift from partial to whole representations. In A. J. Sameroff and M. M. Haith (Eds.), *The five to seven year shift: The age of reason and responsibility* (pp. 85–110). Chicago: University of Chicago Press.

Nelson, K. (1996). Memory development from 4 to 7 years. In A. J. Sameroff and M. M. Haith (Eds.), *The five to seven year shift: The age of reason and responsibility* (pp. 141–160). Chicago: University of Chicago Press.

Piaget, J. (1962). *Play, dreams, and imitation in childhood* (trans. by C. Gattegno and F. M. Hodgson). New York: W. W. Norton.

Piaget, J. (1973). The affective unconscious and the cognitive unconscious. *Journal of the American Psychoanalytic Association, 21,* 249–261.

Piaget, J. (1976). *The grasp of consciousness: Action and concept in the young child* (trans. by S. Wedgwood). Cambridge MA: Harvard University Press.

Piaget, J. and Inhelder, B. (1969). *The psychology of the child* (trans. by H. Weaver). New York: Basic Books.

Piaget, J. and Inhelder, B. (1971). *Mental imagery in the child* (trans. by P. A. Chilton). New York: Basic Books.

Pitcher, E. G. and Prelinger, E. (1963). *Children tell stories: An analysis of fantasy.* New York: International Universities Press.

Ramsey, G. V. (1953). Studies of dreaming. *Psychological Bulletin, 50,* 432–455.

Rechtschaffen, A., Bergmann, B. M., Everson, C. A., Kushida, C. A., and Gilliland, M. A. (1989). Sleep deprivation in the rat: I. Conceptual issues. *Sleep, 12,* 1–4.

Rechtschaffen, A. and Foulkes, D. (1965). Effect of visual stimuli on dream content. *Perceptual and Motor Skills, 20,* 1149–1160.

Resnick, J., Stickgold, R., Rittenhouse, C. D., and Hobson, J. A. (1994). Self-representation and bizarreness in children's dream reports collected in the home setting. *Consciousness and Cognition, 3,* 30–45.

Rittenhouse, C. D., Stickgold, R., and Hobson, J. A. (1994). Constraint on the transformation of characters, objects, and settings in dream reports. *Consciousness and Cognition, 3,* 100–113.

Rosenthal, D. M. (1993). Thinking that one thinks. In M. Davies and G. W. Humphreys (Eds.), *Consciousness* (pp. 197–223). Cambridge MA: Basil Blackwell.

Roussy, F., Camirand, C., Foulkes, D., De Koninck, J., Loftis, M., and Kerr, N. H. (1996). Does early-night REM dream content reliably reflect presleep state of mind? *Dreaming, 6,* 121–130.

Sameroff, A. J. and Haith, M. M. (Eds.) (1996). *The five to seven year shift: The age of reason and responsibility.* Chicago: University of Chicago Press.

Schacter, D. L. (1987). Implicit memory: History and current status. *Journal of Experimental Psychology: Learning, Memory, and Cognition, 13,* 501–518.

Shepard, R. N. and Cooper, L. A. (1982). *Mental images and their transformations.* Cambridge MA: MIT Press.

Snyder, F. (1970). The phenomenology of dreaming. In L. Madow and L. H. Snow (Eds.), *The psychodynamic implications of the physiological studies on dreams* (pp. 124–151). Springfield IL: Charles C Thomas.

Solms, M. (1997). *The neuropsychology of dreams: A clinico-anatomical study.* Mahwah NJ: Lawrence Erlbaum Associates.

Spanos, N. P. (1996). *Multiple identities and false memories: A socio-cognitive perspective.* Washington DC: American Psychological Association.

Squire, L. R. (1986). Mechanisms of memory. *Science, 232,* 1612–1619.

Steriade, M. (1996). Arousal: Revisiting the reticular activating system. *Science, 272,* 225–226.

Stickgold, R. and Hobson, J. A. (1994). Home monitoring of sleep onset and sleep-onset mentation using the Nightcap. In R. D. Ogilvie and J. R. Harsh (Eds.), *Sleep onset: Normal and abnormal processes* (pp. 141–160). Washington DC: American Psychological Association.

Strauch, I. and Meier, B. (1996). *In search of dreams: Results of experimental dream research.* Albany NY: SUNY Press.

Trollope, A. (1859). *The Bertrams.* London: Penguin Books, 1993.

Trupin, E. W. (1976). Correlates of ego-level and agency-communion in stage REM dreams of 11–13 year old children. *Journal of Child Psychology and Psychiatry, 17,* 169–180.

Tulving, E. (1983). *Elements of episodic memory.* New York: Oxford University Press.

Van de Castle, R. L. (1971). *The psychology of dreaming.* New York: General Learning Press.

Van de Castle, R. L. (1994). *Our dreaming mind.* New York: Ballantine.

Vaughan, C. J. (1963). The development and use of an operant technique to provide evidence for visual imagery in the rhesus monkey under "sensory deprivation". Ph.D. dissertation, University of Pittsburgh.

Vogel, G. W. (1978). An alternative view of the neurobiology of dreaming. *American Journal of Psychiatry, 135,* 1531–1535.

Vogel, G. W., Foulkes, D., and Trosman, H. (1966). Ego functions and dreaming during sleep onset. *Archives of General Psychiatry, 14,* 238–248.

Weiskrantz, L. (1997). *Consciousness lost and found.* Oxford: Oxford University Press.

Weisz, R. and Foulkes, D. (1970). Home and laboratory dreams collected under uniform sampling conditions. *Psychophysiology, 6,* 588–596.

White, S. H. (1965). Evidence for a hierarchical arrangement of learning processes. *Advances in Child Development and Behavior, 2,* 187–220.

Winget, C. and Kramer, M. (1979). *Dimensions of dreams.* Gainesville FL: University Presses of Florida.

Index